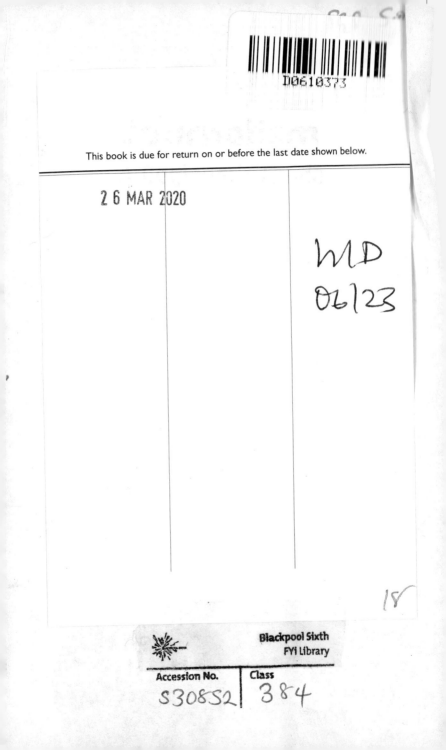

D0610373

This book is due for return on or before the last date shown below.

2 6 MAR 2020

WD
06/23

18

ONEWORLD BEGINNER'S GUIDES combine an original, inventive, and engaging approach with expert analysis on subjects ranging from art and history to religion and politics, and everything in between. Innovative and affordable, books in the series are perfect for anyone curious about the way the world works and the big ideas of our time.

Beginners
GUIDES

Journalism
A Beginner's Guide

Sarah Niblock

ONEWORLD

OXFORD

A Oneworld Paperback Original

Published by Oneworld Publications 2010

Copyright © Sarah Niblock 2010

ISBN 978–1–85168–703–9

Typeset by Jayvee, Trivandrum, India
Cover design by vaguelymemorable.com
Printed and bound in Great Britain by Bell & Bain, Glasgow

Oneworld Publications
UK: 185 Banbury Road, Oxford, OX2 7AR, England
USA: 38 Greene Street, 4th Floor, New York, NY 10013, USA
www.oneworld-publications.com

Learn more about Oneworld. Join our mailing list to
find out about our latest titles and special offers at:

www.oneworld-publications.com

Mixed Sources
Product group from well-managed
forests and other controlled sources
www.fsc.org   Cert no. TT-COC-002769
© 1996 Forest Stewardship Council

Contents

Acknowledgements

I would like to thank my colleague, Professor Julian Petley, for proposing me as the author of this title. I also owe a debt of gratitude to the commissioning editor, Mike Harpley, for his inspiration and close scrutiny during the writing stage. Heartfelt thanks go to copy editor Ann Grand for her detailed attention to the manuscript. On a personal level, I wish to thank Scott and Eloise for their enduring patience during the long hours I spend at my keyboard. I dedicate this book to my students – past, present and future – who care passionately about journalism in all its incarnations. Hopefully, the future of this trade will flourish in their capable hands.

1

From muck-raking to multi-tasking: a brief history of news-making

Human beings have always been curious about the world around them. For most of humankind's existence, people have been anxious to know about events and issues that may have an impact on their lives. From ballads and travellers' tales to the Internet, the public has received its digest of the day's news in many ways, each fuelling our curiosity, our fears, our joys and our hopes. Journalism, put simply, is a form of communication that tells us about events and issues of which we might not already know. The role of a journalist is similarly broad and covers more than just writing and reporting: the realm of journalism covers not only hard news but also documentaries, features, photojournalism, business and commerce and entertainment. Globally, literally hundreds of thousands of people work in the media, in a vast range of roles. Journalists may work as sub-editors, feature writers, columnists, broadcast producers and newsreaders, to name but a few typical occupations. The scope of topics covered by journalists is unlimited and the number of media available to convey their stories is expanding even as the media themselves converge. In the digital age, even the blogger sitting before their computer screen might be seen to be performing some of the functions of a journalist. But that is a contentious view; more on that later. An important characteristic that all good journalists share, whether they work in print, broadcasting or online, is curiosity. Journalists should be driven by a strong compulsion to investigate and mediate information about the world around us.

Journalism is, and always has been, an exciting and controversial industry and one which for centuries has been subject to intense scrutiny of its purposes, practices and standards. Journalism serves many different, and sometimes conflicting, functions and interests. The role of news providers is to unearth facts of public interest and to mediate them for their audience in a neutral way. Thus, the public can make informed judgments of its actions and opinions which may in turn benefit society as a whole. Yet it must not be forgotten that the vast bulk of this diverse and dynamic industry relies on a strong business imperative; news is a commodity that makes profits for shareholders and delivers customers to advertisers. If journalism does not sell, there will not be enough money to fund the next reporting cycle. So journalism has to be attractive to its audiences, to maximise circulations and guarantee a return on its costs. Readers, listeners and viewers need to be engaged by the media if they are to subscribe to its products in sufficient numbers to make them profitable, which means journalism also has a remit to entertain. (By 'entertaining' I do not mean that a newspaper or website has to make its audience laugh out loud; in the context of journalism, 'entertaining' means that content has to be thought-provoking, dramatic, emotive or even provocative, to ensure consumers wish to engage with the product over and over again.)

News today is at the nexus of a range of shifting and sometimes conflicting factors, such as new technology, fierce competition, big-business interests and tightening legal and regulatory frameworks. But none of this is new. The history of journalism reveals a great deal about why the media operate the way they do today. It is possible to trace how gradual developments in mass communications technology, alongside the rise of news-as-business, have formalised the oral transmission of news from community to community into today's carefully-crafted, synchronised, mass media. It also shows that contemporary concerns about sleaze, scandal and scaremongering were as commonplace during journalism's development as they are today.

For example, 'citizen journalism', in which members of the public contribute to the gathering and dissemination of news has been described as a new phenomenon spurred by the easy mass availability of Internet technology. Yet the earliest form of transmitting news was by word-of-mouth. In the prehistory of journalism, news was limited to what people saw and re-told, and its accuracy depended on how close the narrator had been to the scene of the action. Other forms of relaying news included ballads, which often re-told stories of events of the day and – for the literate – letters. The selection of which stories to impart greatly depended then, as now, on the impact the oral report might have on its listener. Gradually, monarchies and governments (such as the Roman Empire under Julius Caesar) developed methods for distributing written daily records of political developments to their colonies. When the Roman Empire collapsed, once again news was relayed informally from person to person and group to group in written and verbal forms, in a similar way to today's blogs and websites.

Eventually, accounts from different sources were written down and distributed in the very earliest forms of news media. One of the earliest newsletters was a handwritten sheet circulated in Beijing, in China. In Renaissance Europe, hand-written newsletters circulated privately among merchants, passing information about everything from wars and economic conditions to social customs and 'human interest' features. Business journalism, fundamental to contemporary practice, originated in these newsletters, the antecedents of that currently burgeoning sector of journalism, the 'trade' or 'business-to-business' press. Among the most popular were the Fugger newsletters, launched by the wealthy Renaissance businessman Jakob Fugger, which were compiled by journalists known as *menanti*. Written in Italian, then the language of commerce, they contained news and information specific to business, such as the decline of the Hapsburg's fortunes. The intention of these newsletters was to promote commercial interests. They are not considered to be 'proper' newspapers as, reliant on primitive reproduction techniques, they were published only infrequently.

The opportunity for wider formal dissemination of news came in 1456, when the German, Johannes Gutenberg, invented the movable type printing press, which allowed printers to set type by hand, one letter at a time. Soon after this development in printing, sheets carrying news made their appearance, as did books, in particular the Bible. The forerunners of the modern newspaper appeared in Germany in the late 1400s, in the form of news pamphlets or broadsides. Pamphlets were cheap one-page opinion papers, often with highly sensational content, which were used to criticise politics and religion. Some of the most famous report atrocities against Germans in Transylvania, perpetrated by the sadistic warlord, Vlad Tsepes Drakul, who became the *Count Dracula* of Bram Stoker's novel.

The first newspapers (in the sense of a recurring publication) did not appear in Europe until the late sixteenth century. The *Mercurius Gallobelgicus* (Cologne, 1592) was the world's first periodical, written in Latin and distributed semi-annually at book fairs. The *Oxford Gazette* (1665) was the first regularly-published newspaper. It began publication at a time when the English court was in Oxford, to avoid the Plague then raging in London. When the court returned to London, the *Gazette* went with it. In America, the first newspaper, entitled *Publick Occurrences*, was published in Boston in 1690. The world's oldest surviving newspaper (first published in 1645), a little-known Swedish title, *Post-och Inrikes Tidningar*, is still in circulation at the time of writing, albeit having just moved to online-only publication.

Even as technical advances enabled the wider dissemination of news and information, they were accompanied by states' attempts to limit freedom of expression. The concept of 'freedom of the press', whereby journalists' reporting of matters of public interest should be unfettered either by governmental or any other outside interference, has become paradigmatic in developed countries, particularly those of the West. However, press censorship was intense on both sides of the Atlantic until at least the late eighteenth century. Typically of many papers in North America, *Publick Occurrences* was immediately suppressed by the government and its publisher arrested for not having a licence. (Licences were only issued to printers if they agreed that their publication would not criticise the authorities – in effect imposing one of the earliest forms of state control of journalism.) A further limit on the power of the press in America came with the 1765 Stamp Act, in which the British colonial government legislated to limit the transfer of documents, such as pamphlets and legal papers, in the colonies of British America. Although technically the legislation only taxed a commodity – paper – the Act was widely viewed as a form of press regulation; newspapers were required to use only newsprint that had been stamped to indicate the tax had been paid. Any newspaper without that stamp could be suppressed. The British government was unprepared for the strength of bitter opposition to this law and the Act was repealed in 1766. This, followed by the ratification of the US Bill of Rights in 1791, at last guaranteed freedom of the press and allowed America's newspapers to take on a central role in national affairs.

Until the nineteenth century, similar – fervently opposed – constraints were imposed throughout Europe, Russia and Asia.

This was also an age of strict press censorship in Japan; its first daily newspaper (1870), the *Yokohama Mainichi*, was born at a time when arrests of journalists and suppression of newspapers were all too common. Colonial governments, such as those of Russia and Britain, exercised a tight control over political publications; the Russians in the Baltic states, the British in Australia, Canada, India and colonial Africa. In Australia, full censorship lasted until 1823, while in South Africa a press law passed in 1828 secured a modicum of publishing freedom. In Britain, the case for freedom of expression was fought philosophically as well as politically through the work of writers such as John Locke, John Milton and, later, John Stuart Mill.

JOHN STUART MILL

The British philosopher John Stuart Mill (1806–1873) played an influential role in defining the balance of power between the state and the people. He produced a significant body of work that straddled a number of disciplines including economics, ethics, politics and religion. Influenced in part by the social reformer Jeremy Bentham (1748–1832), who campaigned for greater equality under the law, Mill was committed to the idea that there should be limits on the power that society can have over the individual. This extended into a major treatise on the notion of freedom from oppression. His 1859 work, *On Liberty*, served as the bedrock for the defence of freedom of the press. In this work, Mill stated that power should be exercised strictly in adherence *to the 'harm principle'* only. This principle entails that:

> … the sole end for which mankind are warranted, individually or collectively, in interfering with the liberty of action of any of their number, is self-protection. That the only purpose for which power can be rightfully exercised over any member of a civilized community, against his will, is to

JOHN STUART MILL (cont.)

prevent harm to others. His own good, either physical or moral, is not a sufficient warrant. He cannot rightfully be compelled to do or forbear because it will be better for him to do so, because it will make him happier, because, in the opinion of others, to do so would be wise, or even right. These are good reasons for remonstrating with him, or reasoning with him, or persuading him, or entreating him, but not for compelling him, or visiting him with any evil in case he do otherwise.

(Mill, J.S. *On Liberty*)

Mill argued passionately for free speech as a necessary condition for political and social progress. Without individual liberty, he argued, we become subject to the tyranny of government, which needs to be controlled by citizens. Governing people by censoring knowledge is ineffective and leads to a general degradation of any society, he argued. By allowing liberty and by extension freedom of speech, Mill asserted that human civilisation would develop and progress.

Whilst overt state control had subsided in some parts of the world by the middle of the nineteenth century, in other places, such as parts of Africa, Russia and Asia, strong curbs persisted and are still present today. However, state oppression encouraged disempowered groups to harness the power of the press to highlight their situation. For example, rampant and flagrant discrimination against African–Americans in the US encouraged black journalists to find a voice in the founding of their own daily and weekly newspapers, particularly in the cities. These newspapers, and other publications, flourished because of the loyalty of their readers at a time of great oppression. The first black newspaper was *Freedom's Journal*, first published on March 16th, 1827 by John B. Russworn and Samuel Cornish.

The power struggle between state and press often became acute during significant technological advances that enabled news to be more freely and speedily circulated. The nineteenth century saw dramatic developments in journalism, which had far-reaching effects as resonant as any of the recent changes wrought by the Internet; major advances in printing and in paper-making technology that led to rapid growth in the newspaper industry and the emergence of mass-circulation newspapers that an ordinary member of the public could afford to buy. Until this time, newspapers were funded by yearly subscription, paid in full and in advance – something only the wealthy élite could afford. However, increasing industrialisation drew people from the country into employment in cities. Thanks to these dramatic political and demographic shifts, and rising literacy levels, newspaper owners found a new market for their products, offering the public an ever-present supply of cheap and interesting reading matter, sold on street corners by newspaper boys.

The emerging economics of mass production and distribution offered news media owners both the beginnings of the profit incentive dominant today and the possibility of breaking free of political control and asserting their independence. (Until this time, most newspapers had been politically partisan, dependent to varying extents on party patronage.) Massive new presses could print thousands of copies of a newspaper every hour to feed these increased circulations, while the emergence of illustrated newspapers offered proprietors the ability to heighten the appeal of their product. The growing public demand for a steady stream of news forced proprietors to develop the first 'professional' and ostensibly objective newsrooms.

Despite the growing interest in international affairs, newspapers were still regional and local until the mid-nineteenth century, largely due to the logistics of production and distribution. Horace Greeley's *New York Tribune,* launched in 1841,

JAMES GORDON BENNETT

The Scottish-born James Gordon Bennett (1795–1872), who launched the *New York Herald* in 1835, took this title from the ranks of the Penny Press to a significant circulation (40,000) in fifteen months. He was among the first proprietors to establish a formal newsroom structure and editorial practices similar to those that operate today. Bennett is associated with the first journalistic interview – the present-day bedrock of news protocols – when the *Herald* led on the shocking and sensational story of the murder of a prostitute, Helen Jewett. He went on to create one of the first foreign desks, featured political interviews and (albeit using woodcuts) ensured that the *Herald* had visual appeal. The modern concept of news as 'immediate' and 'fresh' was important to Bennett: he put journalists on boats to meet foreign ships bringing news from overseas to speed up the time it took to get the information into print.

changed this. The appeal of his title beyond New York was secured by his illustrious staff (which for a short time included the revolutionary socialist thinker Karl Marx) and his campaigning liberalism, which spurred the identification of the journalist as a crusader. Under Greeley's leadership, the *Tribune*, circulated by rail and steamboat lines, became the first newspaper to unite the country, in the mission to abolish slavery. Later, during the American Civil War, Greeley transported thousands of copies of the *Tribune* to other cities. And in 1886, the *Tribune* took a further technological leap by becoming the first newspaper to adopt Ottmar Mergenthaler's linotype machine, rapidly increasing the speed and accuracy with which type could be set. (The linotype machine allowed printers to set a line of type at once, using the machine's 90-character keyboard. Because the one-character-at-a-time Gutenberg process was so slow, for more than 400 years after the press's invention, most newspapers consisted of eight pages or fewer. With the advent of the linotype, that quickly changed.)

As editors overcame logistical problems, they became keen to expand their news coverage. The invention of the telegraph (by Samuel Morse in 1837) boosted the speed and reliability of reporting by enabling the swift transfer of information from one source to another; even from one country to another. A new type of news provider emerged to supply the demand for coverage of international affairs. Major news agencies, known commonly as 'wire' services, originated in France in 1835 with the founding of *Agence Havas*, which later became *Agence France Presse* (AFP). Its founder, Charles-Louis Havas, is described on AFP's website as 'the father of global journalism'. In 1848, six large New York papers set up a co-operative, or pool system, to provide stakeholders with coverage of events in Europe, rather than each newspaper suffering the expense of placing dedicated staff overseas. This arrangement was later formalised into the *Associated Press*, which received the first-ever transmission of European news through the transatlantic cable. Information that had previously taken ten days to be transported by ship between America and Europe could now be transferred in a few minutes.

As technology transformed the speed of newspaper production and lowered its costs, it also permeated the styles of writing and to some extent served to professionalise and formalise the nature of journalism. Because telegraphs often broke down, sometimes a reporter was cut off before they had finished sending their story. To alleviate this, reporters developed the 'inverted pyramid' form, putting the most important facts at the beginning of the story. Thus, the most important part of the story would probably reach the newspaper and if anything did get cut off, it would be the story's least important aspects. Telegraph and cable transmission also required much tighter, more concise sentences and paragraphs, in contrast to the more literary style of earlier newspapers. Journalists had to recount their story in as few words as possible, to pack in the maximum facts. This approach persists in news reporting, not only in newspapers but also in broadcast and online journalism. The reporter gets straight to the crux of the story, spelled out in the first short, attention-grabbing, concise paragraph. Although journalism is a form of storytelling and can employ similar dramatic devices, journalists must not wait to deliver a *dénouement*: the reader has to be told the essential facts at the outset.

Better printing technology and increased transmission speed also enabled newspapers to compete more and more to increase their circulation and obtain more advertising revenue. Charles Anderson Dana of the *New York Sun* (1861), a former editor for Horace Greeley, articulated for the growing industry the now universal description of what makes news: 'man bites dog' not 'dog bites man'. That is, if it is to attract and interest large audiences, news should convey out-of-the-ordinary events rather than the predictable and everyday. An increasingly sensationalist journalism began to emerge, spurred by proprietors' competition for readership. In the mid-1890s, Joseph Pulitzer (in the *New York World*) and William Randolph Hearst (in the *San Francisco Examiner* and later the *New York Morning Journal*) transformed newspapers, with sensational and scandalous news coverage, drawings and features such as comic strips. This type of journalism was labelled 'yellow journalism' after Pulitzer, in early 1896, began publishing colour comic sections that included a strip entitled *The Yellow Kid*. Drawn by R.F. Outcault, the popular strip became a prize in the struggle between Pulitzer and Hearst in the New York newspaper wars. Outcault moved the strip to Hearst's papers after nine months, where it competed with a Pulitzer-sponsored version of itself.

The proliferation of cheap newspapers in the 'yellow journalism' era encouraged the development of a new category of journalists: the 'muck-rakers', who sought to expose corruption in business and government and reveal the wretchedness of life for the new urban poor. One of the most popular muck-rakers was Elizabeth Cochrane, who wrote under the name Nellie Bly. Cochrane felt very strongly that women and their issues were neither represented in newspapers nor anywhere else. She wanted people to recognise women's plights and understand why some became 'fallen women' and hoped that through reading her articles, people would realise the unfairness that women suffered. She wrote with anger and compassion, exposing the many wrongs that existed in the industrial boom cities of the nineteenth century. Most of Cochrane's reporting was on women's issues, and directed towards upper-class women, to open their eyes and hearts to their impoverished sisters. Other muck-rakers included Lincoln Steffens, Ida Tarbell and Upton Sinclair, who shared a strong social conscience and a dedication to uprooting corruption, especially in the practices of big businesses

In 1895, Hearst purchased the *New York Morning Journal* and entered into a head-to-head circulation war with his former mentor, Joseph Pulitzer, owner of the *New York World*. To increase circulation, both started to include articles about the Cuban Insurrection but many stories, in both newspapers, were greatly exaggerated to make the stories more sensational. A major story – that of Señorita Clemencia Arango – which enraged the American public was written by one of Hearst's reporters, Richard Harding Davis, as he returned from Cuba. Arango had been forced out of Cuba for helping the rebels and allegedly, during her deportation, was strip-searched by male Spanish detectives, which angered the sensibilities of the American public. Eventually the story was found to be wrong: women had searched Arango, not men.

The challenge of broadcast journalism to the print industry

The technology that enabled the mass circulation of popular newspapers enabled a further major transformation of the media industry in the early part of the twentieth century. The development of wireless radiotelegraphy by Gugliemo Marconi spearheaded the growth of a new medium – radio – that would close the gap between the listener and real-world events. Journalism's status and penetration was enhanced as radio, and later television, metaphorically transported the listener to the scene and allowed them to hear events and speakers at first hand. In the USA, the first actual radio broadcast took place in 1912 in Los Angeles, but regular broadcasts did not happen until the emergence of the first US radio station, KDKA in Pittsburgh, in 1920. NBC began operations in 1926, followed by CBS the next year. Early broadcasts included election and sports results; in the 1930s, President Franklin Delano Roosevelt demonstrated the ability of the new medium to allow direct communication with the public through his 'fireside chats', broadcast nationally on the developing radio networks.

In Britain, the public service broadcaster, the British Broadcasting Company (later Corporation), began daily radio broadcasts in 1922. According to its first Director-General, John Reith, the BBC was a public service, whose mission was to inform and educate on all that is best in human endeavour, knowledge and achievement. This public service status was in direct contrast to the business model that funded print journalism, and safeguarded journalistic independence from external or commercial influence. Funded through licence fees (under which arrangement each television-owning household must pay a set annual amount to receive terrestrial broadcasts), the BBC's independence is guaranteed by its status as neither government department nor commercial company.

Unlike newspapers, radio (and later television) was subject to government regulation of content. In the US, the Federal Radio Commission, which in 1934 became the Federal Communication Commission, required broadcast outlets to obtain a licence, the retention of which was dependent on demonstrating that the stations provided for the public good. In the UK, the BBC must adhere to the provisions of its Royal Charter, under which it is required to be free from both political and commercial influences and to answer only to its viewers and listeners.

Just as the American Civil War inaugurated the high-speed transmission of news from remote areas through the telegraph system, World War II established the power of radio as a news medium. The Prime Minister, Winston Churchill, in Britain and President Roosevelt in the USA used radio broadcasts to rally their citizens, while intrepid radio reporters, such as Edward Murrow of CBS, brought the actuality of the war directly into people's homes. By 1929, pictures had joined sound, as the first experimental television broadcasts were made. The full development of television was delayed by the Second World War, and powerful news and entertainment networks only began to emerge in the 1950s. The BBC had a monopoly on British television news until 1954, when commercial services were launched, including news and current affairs bulletins provided by Independent Television News (ITN). ITN was owned collectively by the regional ITV companies and run on a non-profit-making basis. So successful was its output that ITN won the contract to supply the fourth UK terrestrial service, Channel 4, launched in 1981. As well as ITN's London-based services, the commercial providers were committed to broadcasting regional news and current affairs programming. But the shift from local to global broadcast news, which transformed the journalistic landscape for UK and US audiences, was rapid from the 1980s onwards.

In 1980, the American media entrepreneur Ted Turner's company broke new ground with the launch of CNN, the first 24-hour all-news network, which changed forever the way the world saw breaking news. Today, CNN reaches nearly one billion people around the globe. It had a major global impact with the immediacy of its coverage of the first Gulf War (1990–91), although its audience in the UK was relatively small at that time. In 1989, Rupert Murdoch changed the face of British broadcasting by launching Sky News, the UK's domesti-cally-produced 24-hour satellite news network. The 'rolling news' format is not without its controversies and critics. For example, its critics argue that the pressure to keep information on screen means there is little time to check facts before they are broadcast. Whereas newspapers might have time to clarify, correct and put breaking stories into context, rolling news puts out snippets of information as they happen, meaning the audience has to interpret and order the information itself. There has also been criticism of a possible tendency to exploit the visual nature of incidents to sensational effect. It has been claimed, for instance, that CNN portrayed the first Gulf War as a pyrotechnic event, to heighten the televisual drama and maximise audiences, a claim they vigorously refute. Whatever the truth, there are concerns that rolling news has the potential to reduce news to a visual spectacle, as opposed to it being unpacked, analysed and journalistically-mediated.

As broadcast news has become the dominant outlet for breaking news, the print news medium has constantly sought new formats to attract readers. In the 1960s, originally in the underground press but then in more mainstream outlets, a 'New Journalism' emerged, which combined traditional reporting with more creative, literary methods of telling stories that included elements borrowed from fiction. The term originated in 1887, coined by Mathew Arnold to describe W.T. Stead's writing in the *Pall Mall Gazette*. In contrast to the aura of objectivity that had come to be seen as the grail of mainstream reporting, 'New Journalism' often called attention to the journalist as a not-completely-unbiased observer, as in Hunter S. Thompson's reporting for *Rolling Stone*. What distinguished 'New Journalism' practitioners in the 1960s and 1970s was not that they were doing anything different but that so many were doing it simultaneously. In his book, *The New Journalism* (1973), Tom Wolfe rejected the notion that the reporter's tone should be impersonal or that the sense of the writer's presence be underplayed so as not to alienate readers: 'When they came across that pale beige tone, it began to signal them, unconsciously, that a known bore was here again, "the journalist," a pedestrian mind, a phlegmatic spirit, a faded personality, and there was no way to get rid of the pallid little troll, short of ceasing to read.'

The convention of journalism was to inform audiences and allow them to form their own judgements based on 'truths'; Wolfe and his contemporaries sought to present a more detailed, descriptive picture. To do otherwise, they argued, was to present the reader with an incomplete representation. In a sense, New Journalism might be seen as trying to cultivate the senses in the same way as the broadcast media, transporting the audience to the scene of events. While it might appear, as for example in the work of Truman Capote, that the focus is on literary style, this form of journalism came into its own as a methodical system of data collection. One of the main formats for information-gathering by a journalist is the interview: the method favoured by 'new' journalists was shadowing, immersing themselves in the events depicted and imparting the detailed verbal and non-verbal behaviour of the subjects. Wolfe maintained this method ensured a more effective determination of the subjects' genuine character as opposed to an 'objective' façade, adopted for the given moment of the formal journalistic interview.

The 1960s and 1970s saw a reinvigorated media, filled with investigative zeal, which summoned a surge of young people into careers in the news industry. The cultural context of social unrest, the questioning of the *status quo*, the redefinition of roles and the urge for recognition of human rights fostered a scepticism and irreverence which made investigative journalism attractive. The consumer boom of the 1960s meant more advertising, which in turn offered more space for pictures and features. As television and radio began to offer faster access to news, print journalism was forced to reflect on its purpose as a primary news provider. It became increasingly feature-led, offering extended, hard-hitting investigations. Some of the most famous occurred during this era, including the work that led to the revelation that the drug Thalidomide, then widely prescribed to pregnant women, was causing devastating damage to their unborn children (1972 in *The Times*). And the threat to national security of the Profumo affair was researched and revealed by the *News of the World* investigative reporter, Peter Earle, in 1963. The Secretary of State for War, John Profumo, was discovered to be having an affair with Christine Keeler, who was simultaneously in a casual relationship with a Russian spy. Profumo was forced to resign from the government after he lied about the affair to the House of Commons. In the same year, the *Sunday Times* 'Insight' team exposed the landlord Rachman, who used criminal methods to terrify his tenants. They set a trend for what was to follow, from bugging the Metropolitan Police and exposing their corruption to revealing gun-running by the IRA. The trend reached the broadcast media: Granada TV launched *World in Action*, its weekly current affairs programme, in 1963.

By the 1970s and 1980s, conditions were ripe on both sides of the Atlantic for a deeper interrogation of the uses and mis-uses of institutional power and politics. One of the most celebrated moments of crusading journalism was the

Watergate scandal. Carl Bernstein and Bob Woodward, two young reporters on the *Washington Post*, aided by their covert source 'Deep Throat', painstakingly investigated President Nixon's administration, an investigation that led to Nixon's resignation in 1974. The story had a perceptibly positive effect on public opinion of journalists and the news industry, making heroes of the reporters and villains of those in authority who conducted their lives in an unethical manner. Journalism was viewed by its eager recruits as a career that could make a difference and they entered the trade in their droves, despite the fact that Bernstein and Woodward's memoirs do not attempt to hide the monotony and painstaking nature of everyday news activity and research. (Their editor-in-chief, Ben Bradlee, refused to print the Watergate story until every fact was properly and fully validated: a process that took many months.)

New technologies have played a key role in changes in production values and practices that have affected news reporting itself. The invention of desk-top publishing and simple-to-use page make-up software made it easier for journalists to put the news on the page as well as gathering it. Print production processes became speedier and cheaper and many traditional print production roles ended. But alongside this production revolution came a shift in journalism practices, particularly in local and regional journalism, as companies sought to make savings. Reporters worked in much smaller teams and were more often than not office-bound as telephones replaced face-to-face interviews.

Once the computer technology existed that could supplant traditional printing methods, every stage of the production process could be undertaken without the input of traditional print workers: under the 'old' technologies, managers were hugely dependent on several tiers of production workers. In the UK, the printers' unions had had considerable power over

A NEWSPAPER WITHOUT A HOME

In 1982, Al Neuharth, from South Dakota, founded *USA Today* as a national newspaper with no 'home' city. At that time, other than the *Wall Street Journal*, all US newspapers were regional or local. *USA Today* overcame printing and distribution logistics by renting unused time on regional newspaper presses. The paper offered a radical alternative to traditional newspaper fare; homogenised news, with little in-depth or investigative work and was aimed at the 'TV generation'. It devoted little or no coverage to stories taking place outside the USA, and centred its news values on celebrity and sport. It was derided by its rivals for its emphasis on 'infotainment' and human-interest stories but proved to be very influential on both newspaper design and story length. Its bold modular layout resembled the Internet graphics that would follow two decades later. Although initially running at a loss, it began to make significant profits after five years, as advertisers were drawn to the paper by its reader-orientated news values.

newspaper managements, as any dispute could have led to considerable losses of advertising and sales revenues. Rupert Murdoch took the bold step of secretly creating a high-tech news operation next to his new presses in Wapping, in east London. Most of his members of staff at *The Times*, the *Sun* and the *News of the World* were completely unaware of this development until January 1986, when they were informed that their Fleet Street offices were closing. Overnight, amidst huge bitterness, Murdoch transformed his UK operation. Other publishers soon followed suit, albeit with more negotiation with their workforces. Overall, it represented a further major shift in journalism away from staff and towards the interests of the business.

The shape of the journalism industry today

In the latter part of the twentieth century, there was a strong tendency to consolidation. A handful of international and regional media corporations, including AOL-Time Warner, News Corporation, General Electric, Sony, Vivendi, Viacom, Televisa, Globo and Clarín, now control vast sections of the media market. For example, almost 35% of UK newspaper circulation belongs to Rupert Murdoch's News Corporation, while Silvio Berlusconi controls three of Italy's four private broadcasting stations and has recently appointed a friend as head of Italy's public broadcasting station, RAI. This trend towards media concentration is linked to the spread of neo-liberal economics, technological developments and the emergence of global and regional agreements on multi-lateral trade. A corporate media is not necessarily a bad thing, for it can foster healthy competition and provide a check against government power. However, when there is a concentration of ownership there is also a heightened risk that increased economic and political influence can prevail unchecked.

Today, newspapers are an almost US$200 billion industry, employing nearly two million people world-wide. Newspapers fall into one of three main categories; national, regional or local and may be paid-for or free. Major national and regional titles are published daily, either very early in the day (with possibly three or four updated editions following during the morning) or in the afternoon for evening papers; other newspapers are published weekly or bi-weekly. More than 532 million people buy a newspaper every day, up from 486 million in 2003 and average daily readership is estimated to be more than 1.7 billion people. Seventy-four of the world's one hundred best selling daily papers are published in Asia: China, Japan and India account for 62. The five largest markets for daily newspapers are

China (107 million copies), India (99 million copies), Japan (68 million copies), the United States (almost 51 million copies) and Germany (20.6 million copies).

According to figures published annually by the World Association of Newspapers, the total number of paid-for daily newspaper titles jumped over 10,000 for the first time in 2007, to 10,104, a 13% increase since 2001, when there were 8,930 titles. Free daily newspaper circulation more than doubled between 2001 and 2005, from 12 million copies in 2001 to 28 million in 2005, an increase of 137%. However, in the European Union, circulation of paid-for daily newspapers dropped by 2.37% in 2007 alone and dropped by 5.91% between 2003 and 2007. However, when free dailies are counted in, circulation in the EU rose by 2% in 2007 and 9.61% over five years between 2003-2007. The circulation of US dailies fell by 3.03% in 2007 and has fallen by 8.05% since 2003. The picture in Asia was much more positive for the printed press: in 2007, Chinese newspaper sales continued to perform well, up by 3.84% (and by 20.69% over the preceding five years). Indian newspaper sales increased by 11.22% in 2007 and by 35.51% over the preceding five years.

While increased attention has been paid to digital development by newspaper companies, the printed product is also changing. Even in the most developed markets, there has been a proliferation of new genres of newspapers, targeted at new audiences and generating new marketing and distribution scenarios. The surge of new, free titles thrust into the paid-for market is the result of many publishers rethinking the revenue model that has been in place for more than 400 years: is it worth charging the reader for their newspaper when advertisers may have access to more potential purchasers of their products via free papers?

The print industry is also responding to increased competition by reconsidering the distinctions that formerly existed between what is a newspaper and what is a magazine. Because of this, the print newspaper industry has started to adopt a more feature-based style of reporting. Of all print media, the weekly magazine sector has witnessed the biggest growth both in readers and in numbers of titles, many of which contain up-to-the-minute exclusives, even if they are for distinctly specialised readerships. In 2006, in the US alone, 324 new titles were launched. Being such a massive industry, the magazine sector is divided into key categories: consumer magazines, such as women's 'glossy' titles, cater for the mass market general reader, while business and professional titles are aimed at specific markets and are frequently distributed directly rather than sold at news-stands. Other categories of the magazine sector include academic journals, company magazines distributed only to employees and subscriber-only magazines. Magazines have become the most international of all traditional media. The power behind publishing brands has led to expansion into global offices, licensing partnerships and content syndication across several titles within the same company. For example, *Cosmopolitan* magazine, which is targeted at young women, is published in a hundred countries. The brand identity of *Cosmopolitan* is constant and features may be published in more than one of the titles. However, subtle changes may be made to ensure the copy fits local culture, for instance in terms of sexual content. And the magazine model seems to work commercially: the World Advertising Resource Centre estimates that 1.438 billion magazines were sold in 2005, 7.4% (100 million) more than in the previous year.

Broadcasting is poised at an exciting point: viewer and listener choice has increased considerably as new stations and channels, with new formats, have been launched by both commercial and public service broadcasters. Radio, the oldest broadcast medium, is in transition. Listeners are benefiting from a huge increase in the number and range of stations, including community stations, local and national services and, via the Internet, stations around the world, available on a range of platforms, from traditional AM and FM radio to digital radio, digital television and the Internet. And other new technologies will come. However, for established broadcasters, this explosion of choice brings increased competition for listeners and revenues, even as they face the costs of investing in new platforms and deal with competition from an ever-wider range of media. These changes create significant pressures on the traditional pattern of local journalism, which has emerged out of the deliberate public policy of successive governments and regulators: for example, few local stations are required to transmit a dedicated local news service all day.

New technologies have always rapidly transformed the journalistic landscape, in all media, often radically and controversially. Boundaries between different media formats have been breached; news brands compete across several formats. Radio news, once only accessed by tuning in the wireless, is now simultaneously presented on a website, often with video footage or a gallery of images. Browsers of a newspaper's website seeking the latest headlines may see a video bulletin summarising that hour's offerings. Most news operations, from national broadcasters to local newspapers, are putting the Internet at the heart of their operations, re-organising newsrooms and changing the working patterns of their journalists. News organisations started to focus on the Internet in the 1990s, in response to people's increasing use of computers at home and work. US companies were first to venture into publishing newspapers online – the number of US dailies on the web grew from 175 to 750 between 1995 and 1998 – but UK papers soon followed when, in 1994, the *Sunday Times* became the UK's first newspaper with an online edition.

News moved into a novel area in 1997, when the *Dallas Morning News* broke the story that Timothy McVeigh had confessed to the Oklahoma City bombing on the newspaper's website, rather than waiting for the next morning's physical newspaper. The official reason was the story's overwhelming importance but there was also speculation that the decision to release online was made either to prevent a judge from halting publication or to preserve a scoop. McVeigh's lawyers called the story 'a hoax'. The pace of adaptation to the web and multi-format news provision has been rapid, with operations sharing stories, reporters and responsibilities for covering news. Such collaborations have been termed 'crossover coverage' or 'convergence'. Still more recently, we have seen the emergence of blogs and other online-only methods of news transmission. The quality of such vehicles varies widely, as those with an axe to grind take advantage of the Internet's open access to broadcast their views. None the less, from the scoops recorded in the 1990s by the *Drudge Report* to more recent correspondence by politically conservative (but also some liberal) bloggers, the Internet has increasingly become a vehicle for news reports in its own right, not just an adjunct to traditional media.

Conclusion

This abridged journey through the history of journalism has revealed some recurring themes. Journalism occupies a space at the heart of a society and is affected by a range of influences. Time has shown the impact that the prevailing culture can have on journalism practices and how far the business imperative of the journalism industry has played a part: the development of journalistic practices and processes has always been dependent on a business model that ensures wide circulation. The model underlying most journalism has driven news outlets to invest in technology that enables material to be gathered and imparted with as much ease and speed as possible and, most importantly, to the widest-possible audience. The challenge for journalism is to balance business interests against informing the public as fairly and impartially as possible.

2

The news-making process

While journalism is ever-present in our lives, whether we receive it through the medium of the press, broadcasting or mobile devices, few people are able to witness first-hand how news organisations operate. Despite its impact on the lives of millions of people world-wide, the workings of this vast industry remain shrouded in mystery for most. As the digital revolution accelerates and newsrooms scramble to become fully-integrated, journalists of merely ten or twenty years ago would barely recognise the working environment of today's newspaper, magazine or broadcasters' offices. Newsrooms are being re-organised and re-fitted to reflect the arrival of new media forms; traditional roles and job descriptions are becoming outmoded and redundant as editorial staff are required to work across two or more media simultaneously. As the processes of journalism evolve in the ever-more competitive environment of the news business, so does editorial judgement over which stories to include and which to reject.

The twenty-first-century newsroom

Newsrooms across the globe, from small local papers to the giants of broadcasting, have been forced to drastically reorganise the way they operate in response to the demands and challenges of 'multi-platform' or 'converged delivery'. In multi-platform delivery, one media 'brand' produces news in many different ways: a print newspaper may have a website featuring short video reports, or a television station might provide text-based news feeds to mobile telephones.

KNX1070

The KNX1070 news radio station, which serves the Los Angeles area, is a branch of the CBS radio network. It broadcasts in the traditional sense, over the airwaves, but its journalists work simultaneously on several platforms and its website (www.knx1070.com) is a portal to various modes of delivery. Listeners can receive the station on a standard radio but web users can listen live over the Internet, read the news as text with still images, watch video reports on demand or sign up to have the news texted to their mobile phone. In the site's features section, journalists provide background details to the items they can cover only briefly on air

When newsrooms first started to develop a web presence, in the mid 1990s, they kept a clear organisational division between the print or broadcast operation and its upstart online sibling. In print journalism, the newspaper team tended to be dominant and the online group re-packaged their work for the web. The online operation was seen by some editorial managers as a supplement to the printed paper; more of a marketing device than a news service in its own right. That has been over-turned: major newspapers operate a 'web-first' policy, rather than saving the best stories for the printed paper; broadcasters publish simultaneously on the web and on air and send updates to mobile telephones. Likewise, newsrooms have converged: online and 'traditional' media teams either work side-by-side or as one integrated unit.

Key journalistic roles are also being re-organised: journalists must be proficient in one or more media and may have to gather

'PLATFORM-NEUTRAL' NEWSPAPERS

Guardian News & Media integrated its print and online operations, the *Guardian*, the *Observer* and *guardian.co.uk*, when it moved to new premises at Kings Cross, in the heart of London. The space is ultra-modern: white walls, floor–to-ceiling windows overlooking Regent's Canal and designer chairs and sofas scattered around the newsrooms to create zones for informal sharing of ideas.

'Platform-neutral' is one of the key terms of the new newsroom, which was planned for four years before the move and long before the economic downturn. Over the one-and-a-half floors the newsroom occupies, the layout is organised by subject, rather than platform. Heads of national news, international news, business and sport from newspapers and the website sit together and make joint decisions about how stories will be covered in print, online, video and audio formats, rather than taking responsibility for one specific medium. Journalists are grouped, by area of specialisation – for example health, education, politics or media and technology – into 'pods', which publish autonomously straight on to the website. Pods range from five to twenty-eight people and usually include reporters, newspaper sub-editors, website editors and a platform-neutral head. For example, the political journalists work in one pod, report-ing to the head of politics, who covers all platforms and decides which stories to follow and who will cover them. Likewise, the arts journalists sit together, in an area known as the 'culture hub'.

Guardian journalists have access to seven recording studios and 24 video-editing desks. The pictures desk is fully integrated across the three platforms and most of the photographers and many reporters are now trained to produce video. Video production is being taken seriously: in 2008 the *Guardian* was the first newspa-per to win a Royal Television Society award.

and edit video and audio as well as write text or scripts. This is a major transformation, brought about by the ease–of–use, speed and accessibility of new digital software. Technical staff, such as sound editors, whose skills once needed years of training and experience, are being replaced by journalists. Radio bulletins that once needed a small production army to drive the mixing desk while the reader read their script can now be produced by one journalist in a self-operation booth.

Media outlets are being streamlined: content is commissioned from freelancers and journalists are employed shift-by-shift as casual workers or on rolling, short-term contracts that might last a few weeks. News organisations are contracting-out key functions, such as sub-editing or production, to overseas companies. These changes – much more cost-effective than keeping a permanent staff – have benefits and drawbacks. They benefit the organisations, because they can call upon experts as they need them and ensure a range of voices is heard in their publication or website but the disadvantages are that it can be hard for a remote sub-editor to check local facts easily and what is produced can seem distant and impersonal when it is written by people with no real connection to the newspaper or its readers.

The key newsroom roles

The structure of a newsroom varies widely according to the scale of the media operation. Certain roles exist in most newsrooms, with the number of people in each role dependent upon the scale of the editorial operation.

Journalists are independent types, who have to be proactive and self-directed, gathering plenty of stories and features, audio, video and photographs but they also are part of a carefully timed and controlled team. Whether the newsroom comprises five journalists or 500, everyone must perform their function properly and to strict time limits if the operation is to run smoothly. One person running behind their deadline can cost an organisation dearly in missed press time or a package not being ready for broadcast.

The editor-in-chief or chief-of-staff has overall responsibility for the content of the outlet. Editors decide editorial policy, manage the production of publications and the staff involved, determine the content of publications or news items and read and correct material for publication. With other senior editors, they make decisions about running order of material, where it should be placed and how it should be illustrated or accompanied by sound and/or video. This decision-making happens at news conferences, several of which take place during a news cycle (the time it takes to produce a newspaper or bulletin). The editor's role in providing the content of the outlet depends on how well-staffed the organisation is. Editors of smaller local newspapers may also be the main writer and production person. In larger outfits, the editor may be confined to writing the editorial column, because a significant part of their role is to manage the day-to-day running of the outlet, which can mean adhering to a tight budget for staff and production costs. In a very large organisation, the editor may delegate or share some of these editorial and managerial tasks with one or more deputy or assistant editors.

Depending on the size of the organisation, under these senior staff work several section editors – covering divisions such as news, features and sport – with overall responsibility for intake. (Intake refers to the gathering of stories and the production of the necessary text, audio, images or video to support them.) Section editors are middle management, assigning reporters and writers to specific tasks and commissioning freelance journalists. They collaborate closely with the editor-in-chief and senior production staff to ensure that their work is calibrated carefully against the production cycle of the outlet. In a big operation, such as a daily national newspaper or a major broadcaster, sections are likely to be further subdivided into 'desks': news might include a business desk, an entertainments desk, a foreign desk and a series of specialist and general reporters; features might include fashion and lifestyle, reviews, motoring, travel and general feature writers who produce background articles responding to whatever might be in the news. The composition of the desks may change, depending on what audiences want to know – some outlets may not have a celebrity desk but focus instead on arts reviews. At one time, lots of newsroom resources were directed at environment desks but recently these resources have been shifted towards business and personal finance.

Section editors co-ordinate a team of reporters, which is supplemented by a bank of freelances. Reporters and freelances work, under their section editor's instructions, on stories coming in from news agencies, from 'feeds' or breaking in other media. They also generate their own stories, ideally as exclusive reports for their outlet. News journalists generally see their role as finding, reporting and presenting stories that inform, engage and, to some extent, entertain the audience about matters that may affect them. Journalists are often attracted to the job because they enjoy writing but the literary-minded can be disappointed when they discover that the writing often happens in very limited time and uses only the simplest language. Unless the writer has the privilege of being a columnist or works in an area of journalism that permits lengthy prose, most of their time is spent on the telephone or out speaking to contacts. However, this can be one of the most satisfying parts of the reporter's role, particularly if it involves breaking an exclusive story or being 'on the spot' as history unfolds.

Feature writers prepare longer articles, which provide background information and put the news into context. If a plane crashes, while news reporters follow the latest leads and interviews, feature writers produce background pieces about the make of aircraft involved and the history of recent air disasters. Feature writers also prepare articles on non-news topics, such as lifestyle features, profile interviews, reviews or how-to guides. These longer articles balance the short, sharp nature of news

CNN

CNN, the Cable News Network, is a vast US-based international multi-platform news provider. Established by Ted Turner in the 1980s, it started as an influential – and sometimes controversial – 24-hour rolling news channel. It was credited with creating the 'CNN Effect' when social scientists claimed to detect evidence that 24-hour channels were having an impact on governments' policy-making in wartime.

CNN is now produced by staff in London and Hong Kong, who work with colleagues at CNN's world headquarters in Atlanta, Georgia and bureaux world-wide. Its continuously-updated website (www.CNN.com) relies heavily on CNN's global team of more than 4,000 news professionals. CNN.com/International features the latest multi-media technologies, from live video streaming to audio packages to searchable archives of news features and background information.

This huge structure has many different sub-sections, or 'desks' as they are commonly known in journalism. For example, the international website has desks covering the US, Asia, Europe, world business, technology, entertainment and world sport.

with in-depth extended writing or investigation and serve as light-hearted relief from hard news.

Once the text has been written and the images and audio gathered, the information needs to be edited before publication or broadcast. This is known as sub-editing and includes proof-reading, writing headlines and designing pages for print or checking copy in some major broadcast organisations. Traditionally, sub-editing was done by a separate section of editorial staff, dedicated to production as opposed to reporting but the role is now sometimes subsumed within the general editorial role. A radio station's sub-editing might be performed by the duty editor, who checks the scripts adhere to the style and tone of the station. Whoever performs the role of sub-editor, the job entails fact-checking and ensuring the content is legally sound and reads clearly with no mistakes in spelling, grammar or punctuation. In print and online journalism, sub-editing also entails some laying-out, using desk-top publishing software, Sub-editors must have an eye for the visual identity of the outlet and ensure that text and pictures fit well together and are correctly captioned. They also produce the headlines, though the front pages will usually be created in close consultation with other senior journalists, including the editor.

These key production roles are changing drastically and new functions have been created as technology and audience's expectations both change. Newspapers rarely employed designers until the widespread adoption of on-screen page make-up software in the mid to late 1980s. Until then, design had been seen as a distraction from the content; as a visual distraction from the quality of the news. Sub-editors were trades-people, not artists

DESIGNING BRAND IDENTITY

In 2005, a Romanian design company, Grapefruit, was commissioned to develop a design for a national newspaper, *Gândul* (The Thought). The design team was asked to create a blueprint that, through its choice of typefaces and other design features, would convey the newspaper's values. *Gândul* was meant to be an incisive, quality newspaper: Grapefruit created a simple, elegant identity, with a masthead based on an icon familiar to all Romanians, the statue of *The Thinker*. The pages were sized halfway between a broadsheet and a tabloid for ease of reading and the typefaces were selected for ease of reading and legibility. The text on each page was aligned to the left and colour and graphics were used sparsely, to create a modern feel fitting the modern editorial aims of the paper.

and designers and stuck to quite conservative blueprints for page layout. As audiences became increasingly familiar with the design-led approach of advertising and marketing, which had filtered into the magazine sector, newspapers started to employ or commission the services of design editors to develop style guides.

The link between branding and revenue

The growing interest in design-led news production is one part of the increasing influence of branding identity on editorial judgement. Audiences are drawn to the news outlets that accord with their personal values and aspirations and this in turn helps attract advertisers. Newspapers, magazines, websites and commercial broadcasters rely on advertising revenue as an essential component of their economic survival. Paid-for newspapers and magazines receive only a fairly small amount of revenue from the cover price or subscriptions; glossy magazines could not cover their production costs through sales alone; commercial broadcasters, websites and free-distribution newspapers rely on advertising as their sole source of revenue. This explains why advertising and sales are major departments in any editorial enterprise, with large teams offered huge incentives to sell space or airtime at rates linked to prominence.

As more and more outlets compete for a slice of the advertising cake, they have to use highly sophisticated techniques to maintain their market position. News organisations can no longer rely on their reputation alone to attract audiences. In a consumer society, news is a product like any other, which must sell itself to readers, viewers, listeners and browsers. Media companies use branding techniques to illuminate their distinctiveness: by giving their news operation an 'identity', not unlike a car, perfume or pair of trainers, they can more effectively target a specific demographic category of audience. This helps in two ways; first, journalists know exactly who they are trying to reach, so news items, language and images can be chosen with exactly that person in mind. Second, advertising revenues can be maximised, as the advertiser knows they are penetrating their target market.

A good way to find out to what audience a media outlet is appealing is to examine its 'advertiser pack', otherwise known as a media pack, which can usually be found on the outlet's website. For example, the *New York Times*'s website (www.nytimes.whsites.net/mediakit/newspaper/audience/inde x.php) contains links to reader profile surveys of its audience. As competition for advertising revenue becomes fierce, organisations invest large sums of money in thoroughly researching their market, learning about their income, their educational background, their lifestyles and their likes and dislikes, from food, to television programmes, to music. The *New York Times*'s audience profile shows that the majority of its readers are women over 35 years old, college-educated, with an annual income over $100,000 and who own a home worth more than $300,000. Significantly, it is read by large numbers of a group known as the 'influentials'. This title derives from a highly-praised book, *The Influentials*, written by the NOP World executives Ed Keller and Jon Berry. Keller and Berry termed as 'Influentials' the small but persuasive segment of the population that leads social and marketplace trends, shapes public opinion and generates the 'buzz' that increasingly drives consumer behaviour. The *New York Times* offers advertisers different reader profiles for its newspaper, its magazine and its website. Research into the online habits of its web users is provided for advertisers as an inducement:

> Behavioral Targeting offers you the ability to reach niche audiences based on readers' demonstrated interest wherever

they are on NYTimes.com. By utilizing this premium-targeting tool, you can exponentially increase the number of opportunities to reach your niche audience. Experience more efficient use of marketing budgets, expanded ad placement opportunities and increased media impact and effectiveness.

How it works: NYTimes.com collects anonymous data on user behavior on the site. We can track broad behaviors – like visits to particular sections – and narrow ones – like reading about a particular topic or demonstrated interest in luxury real estate. With this data, interest segments are built which can be a key component of a plan running on NYTimes.com.

> www.nytimes.whsites.net/mediakit/online/
> audience/audience_targeting.php

This suggests that Internet sites, which have been viewed as a means to break the top-down approach of 'traditional' media, might in fact be working even more in the interests of advertisers. In a similar way to the *New York Times*, the National Magazine Company – at the time of writing the biggest digital publisher for women in the UK – publisher of high-distribution consumer magazines, including *Cosmopolitan*, promotes its advertising cross-platform to maximise its effective targeting of specific types of readers: 'The team has an expert understanding of consumer behaviour and provides tailored solutions that meet advertiser objectives and harness the combined power of NatMag's print and digital brands.' (www.natmags.co.uk/index.php/v1/About_NatMag_eNgage)

How much an outlet can charge for advertising depends on a number of factors. The prevailing economic conditions will determine a rate that is competitive with other rival media organisations; production costs, such as full-colour advertising, also affect the price. One of the reasons newspapers have added more sections is to increase the amount of space they can sell for advertising, as well as satisfy their readers' interest. The vast range of genres covered, from the arts to motoring, ensures that advertisers can select space they feel best attracts their typical customer, which may explain why the revenues of the quality press, on both sides of the Atlantic, appear to fare a little better than those of the tabloid sector.

Branding has had a significant effect on journalistic content. There has been a growth in lifestyle-oriented journalism that reinforces the brand identity and story angles seek to emphasise the personal and the emotive in hard news stories in a way that was once the preserve of glossy consumer magazines.

NEWS AS FEATURE

On May 31, 2009, the Indian news provider the *Asian Age* ran a story about the recently-inaugurated American President Barack Obama visiting New York (www.asianage.com/presentation/ leftnavigation/news/ international/first-couple-on-a-date-in-new-york.aspx). Rather than reporting on policy issues, the main angle of the article was that Obama was taking his wife, Michelle, on a date in the city. The story described how they had dinner, followed by a trip to the theatre. The upbeat tone of the light-hearted piece concluded with the description of the cheers of onlookers who were surprised to see the pair acting like any other married couple.

Categories of news and features have blurred; page three of many mid-market and quality newspapers, once the preserve of the second-hardest news story of the day, is now often picture-led and time-independent. Susan Boyle, a previously-unknown middle-aged woman from Scotland, who in June 2009 became an international phenomenon on the British television competition *Britain's Got Talent*, made page three of several newspapers because of her distinctive appearance and the human-interest value of her quest for stardom. Such shifts in style and format serve to create a closer rapport with a target audience and are a significant leap from the rather more aloof, top-down and distant tone the media once adopted.

The benefits of this change are two-fold, according to editors, who claim that this represents a democratisation of journalism and makes a much more efficient use of resources by using the stories that cohere with the brand. Thus, they are much more closely in touch with their audiences, responding to what the audience wants, rather than telling them what they should deem important. However, from another perspective, there are serious implications for news journalism when it is produced for a branded product. The *Daily Mail* is a strong and unique brand, offering a hugely-successful package, which, its editor Paul Dacre insists, reflects what his readers are feeling. It could be argued that this is evidence of a shift away from impartial debate and inquiry, reflecting a range of viewpoints towards a singularly-branded ideology. If so, this does not seem to be in the public interest, particularly when the news media are in so few hands.

Brand identity is one of several determinants that help editors decide what to publish and broadcast. When we think of journalism, we tend to think of hard-hitting headlines and breaking stories: in fact, journalism covers a much broader spectrum of genres, forms and formats from printed news to online specialist services, all carefully targeted.

The development of a news story?

Definitions of 'news' commonly refer to 'reports of recent happenings'; to 'facts not previously known'. Yet ask most journalists how they would explain what is newsworthy – the term used by editorial staff to describe any event or issue worthy of coverage – and they would say there are no hard-and-fast rules. After years of working in journalism, reporters and editors barely need to think for a split second: their judgement happens in an instant. Journalists become inculcated with newsroom values and protocols, so that editorial decision-making is almost instant and feels instinctive.

News is often split into one of two types: hard news stories are those most likely to affect the lives of readers directly. They may involve officialdom, politics or the law, determination of how the local area or the country is run or be about conflicts at home and abroad. Crime has a high profile in hard news, as do the activities of the emergency services. Soft (or human interest) news might not directly affect many lives but none the less engages readers emotionally. These stories might be about human endeavour or be offbeat tales about animals, famous people or random unexpected events. Most news organisations

HARD AND SOFT NEWS

On May 18, 2009, the *Los Angeles Times* ran a series of hard and soft news stories on the Californian/local page of its website www.latimes.com. The lead story was that an earthquake, measuring 4.7 on the Richter scale, had struck the city earlier that day. This was a hard news story, containing reports from the emergency services and eyewitnesses. The website featured photographs, some submitted by readers, of earthquake damage and an interactive earthquake 'primer', which provided an informative background to the science of these natural occurrences. The second lead on the site was a news story about the work of a university academic who spent several nights a week tracking down a very elusive beetle. This was a soft news story, of no immediate import to readers but interesting in its own right. Next came another hard news story about California's governor Arnold Schwarzenegger visiting communities as part of his pre-election campaign. Further on, this hard news story was balanced by a softer, human interest story about the First Lady Michelle Obama's visit to a university.

try to strike a balance between hard and soft news, to provide the audience with variety in tone and give their output light and shade.

The best place to start unravelling how journalists select news stories from the vast array of available information is to unpack the very words themselves. The first three letters of 'NEWS' reinforce the proximity of the event or issue to the time it is mediated. To be newsworthy, an event or issue should be *new* to the audience. If it happened a while ago, the facts must be just emerging. Then there is 'STORY'. Journalists must be able to see not just what is happening but also the potential for a strong, exciting narrative that will attract the viewer or listener and compel them to concentrate to the end. So, deciding what to broadcast or publish is commonly a process of rejection rather than selection. The massive growth in public relations, coupled with a steady supply of suggestions from the public and freelance journalists, ensures that news desks have more stories available to them than they could possibly ever handle.

Therefore, journalists ask questions to identify the best content. One of the first will be whether it involves human beings. Stories about people are those everyone, no matter what our personal background, can empathise with. If a new factory is opening in our area, we want to know how many jobs will be created, not whether it is using a pioneering piece of machinery (though a specialist publication may use this as a secondary angle). Events involving death, injury or survival are newsworthy because of the value individual people place on human life. Children and elderly people make compelling subject matter, due to our impulse to protect more vulnerable members of society.

Events and issues involving people are abundant, so journalists need to distil the story's prospects by asking a further question: what is the scale of the event? The greater the number of people affected directly or potentially by an incident, the more chance it will attract an audience. Scale might also apply to money, particularly if someone has won – or stolen – a large sum. Journalists also ask whether the event is unexpected: if an event happens out of the blue, it takes us by surprise and evokes an emotional response. Unfortunately, this news value determines why much of what we hear or read is bad news, for it covers events such as natural disasters, major accidents, wars and terrorist attacks. A significant proportion of news is predicted and planned for: murder trials, sporting events, government budget statements and film premières, but this leaves a vast quantity of potential news items for journalists to sift through. So a fourth question is usually the decider when it comes to ruthlessly selecting the most pertinent items: is it relevant to the target audience?

Relevance in journalism can apply to factors such as geographical location, sex, occupation, age and interests. A local weekly newspaper is unlikely to cover a war overseas, unless a serviceman or woman from their area is killed or performs an act of heroism. A national broadcaster is unlikely to cover a street robbery, unless the victim or their circumstances are of particular interest, such as a celebrity or a very elderly person. An engineers' magazine is unlikely to run a lead story on a medical breakthrough, unless it involves a piece of new machinery. All news outlets have a clearly-demarcated target audience and they won't publish or broadcast anything that does not appeal to that market.

Once a news story has been identified as a likely prospect, the journalist sets to work. They identify sources, carry out interviews, consider legal and ethical issues and set about writing and packaging the story for publication or broadcast. Facts must be checked carefully to ensure the report's veracity. Where information comes from dominates journalists' working lives: a journalist may have a fascinating tip-off about an exclusive story but if they cannot acquire the essential information or eyewitness interviews to back it up, they are not in a safe position to mediate the story to the public. A contacts book is a journalist's most guarded possession; it contains the names, address and other contact details of people who can comment on any issues or events they cover. The contacts might be business leaders, local authorities, politicians, emergency services, charities, schools, hospitals, government departments, celebrities, scientists, pressure groups or more. Journalists spend a good deal of time cultivating their contacts, so they can be the first to obtain the story. The relationship between the journalist and their source is double-edged: the journalist needs the story and the contact is likely to want publicity for their cause. There is potential for exploitation on both sides but the more mutual trust that can be observed the more useful and productive the relationship is likely to be.

Personal interviews, conducted either face-to-face or on the telephone, are the main way journalists get their information. Even when the story comes another way, such as in a letter, the journalist must still speak to the people involved to check the facts and 'flesh out' the details to make interesting, lively copy. It is important for the journalist to direct the conversation so that they can gather the details they require quickly and are not driven off the point by a more experienced or forceful subject, something which can happen when sources, such as politicians, are trained in media skills. Even the most experienced interviewers prepare before speaking to their source, looking at previous stories to which they have contributed and writing and rehearsing the questions in advance.

The questions that are essential for any news story are identified by the 'five Ws and one H': the journalist's formula for getting the complete story. Who: who was involved?; What: what happened, what's the story?; When: when did it happen?; Where: where did it happen?; Why: why did it happen?; How: how did it happen? These 'Five Ws (and one H)' were immortalised by Rudyard Kipling in his *Just So Stories* (1902);

the poem accompanying the tale of *The Elephant's Child* opens with:

> I keep six honest serving-men
> (They taught me all I knew);
> Their names are What and Why and When
> And How and Where and Who.

The questions have to be tailored to fit the story: who is raising the petition; where exactly will the supermarket be built; when are you planning to release your next album? However, these questions tend to elicit a closed response; a simple factual answer or even just 'yes' or 'no', whereas a good interview uses a mixture of closed-ended and open-ended questions, which solicit opinions or feelings. If interviewing the head of a local police force after a bomb blast a journalist would ask closed-ended and basic factual questions to establish precisely what happened. What time did the explosion happen? How many people were injured? Have you identified any suspects? To make the report more dramatic and to help transport the reader to the scene, the journalist would also ask some open-ended questions: what went through the police officer's mind when they heard the blast? How are the victims' families reacting?

When it comes to writing the story, three important rules stay at the forefront of the journalist's mind: the ABCs of journalism – accuracy, balance and concision. *Accuracy* is essential, ethically and legally. If a report contains factual inaccuracies, the journalist and their organisation may be sued for defamation or prosecuted under laws that ensure fair trials. Even a slightly mis-spelled name can damage a journalist's integrity and their relationship with their contacts, making them appear careless of the information entrusted to them.

News, in most contexts, is meant to offer a *balanced* and unbiased picture and give both sides a chance to put their view.

A story which only offers one side will feel unbalanced and lack authority. This can present dilemmas when a newspaper is about to publish an exposé of a public figure. They will often wait until the very last moment before contacting the subject of the story for a comment, in case the subject tries to take out a court injunction to delay publication. Some issues are so highly emotive that it can be difficult for journalists to detach themselves and report impartially. On political issues, newspapers are freer to take an editorial standpoint, as it is felt that readers can choose whether or not to buy that specific title. Broadcast regulation, in most countries, requires strict impartiality in accordance with their public service remit.

The third rule, *concision*, is vital both for the audience and the news outlet. Tightly-paced writing with no verbosity ensures that the information can be absorbed and understood swiftly and unambiguously. Using few adverbs and adjectives and keeping sentences and paragraphs to-the-point, with no extraneous vocabulary, allows more space for quotations and factual detail. For the outlet, concision means more space for other stories, allowing breadth and variety of coverage. This is why journalists use very little punctuation or capitalisation within sentences, as they slow reading time and the flow of broadcast news: instead of writing 'Jane Smith, who works as the Director of Education in Bigtown, replied by commenting …', the journalist would concisely state: 'Bigtown education director Jane Smith said …'

If language must be clear and concise, it follows that the content of the story must be well-organised and simple to understand. This clarity is achieved by ordering information so that, from the outset, the reader or listener is certain what the main point of the issue or event is. The most important paragraph in a news story is the introduction. This must convey – in around 17–25 words – the most significant aspect of the story. It will contain what journalists refer to as the 'angle', the narrative standpoint on which the rest of the story is based. The angle grabs the reader's attention, so it must be selected (possibly from several different approaches) to fit the target audience's expectation.

DIFFERENT ANGLES FOR DIFFERENT AUDIENCES

The US car manufacturer General Motors filed for bankruptcy on June 1, 2009, an event reported in different ways by the news media depending on their target audience and brand identity. The trade magazine *Industry Week* (www.industryweek.com/articles/gm__declares_bankruptcy_19264.aspx?SectionID=7) led the story with the angle that eleven car plants were likely to close, in keeping with their remit to provide an overview of developments in the manufacturing sector. In contrast, the regional evening newspaper the *Liverpool Echo* led on the angle that employees' union leaders were trying to save the jobs of thousands of workers at the Vauxhall (a subsidiary of General Motors) Ellesmere Port car factory, which lies within the *Echo's* readership catchment area. This fits with the over-riding concerns of local readers, more interested in the human cost of the threatened closure than the general global manufacturing position (www.liverpoolecho.co.uk/liverpool-news/local-news/2009/06/01/union-boss-tony-woodley-calls-on-government-to-protect-ellesmere-port-vauxhall-jobs-100252–23759429).

Journalists can find themselves in conflict with one another and with people outside their trade in determining the validity of the invisible criteria used to make far-reaching decisions about what the public gets to know. Academics and media critics argue that there is too much emphasis on celebrity, sport or certain types of crime; most editors would say that their decision to put a particular story at the top of their news bulletin or on the front page of their website is based on careful research about what their target audience wants to read or hear about. There is no escaping the fact that the news industry in the twenty-first century is, first and foremost, a business. The corporate nature of the news business can be seen both in the increased pressure on news outlets to deliver a quality product at reduced cost and in the rise of corporate public relations as a major news source.

The drop in advertising revenue since the end of the twentieth century has coincided with the challenge of new technology. Rather than invest heavily in news budgets to preserve journalistic quality, media owners have sought to diversify their range of outlets to capture – or at least retain – advertising revenue. This, trades unions have claimed, has been at the expense of journalistic practices and working conditions. Fierce commercial objectives, coupled with strong competition for a limited pool of advertisers, has at best resulted in proprietors keeping a tight rein on newsroom budgets. At worst, journalists are working in smaller and smaller teams with more space and air time to fill.

A 2007 survey of regional newspaper journalists in the UK, conducted for the National Union of Journalists, repeatedly heard of staff being forced to do much more work to produce online video and podcasts for no more pay and without proper training. Journalists say their workloads have increased because they are required to do far more with smaller staffs. Less time for information-gathering and fact-checking by journalists raises concerns about editorial integrity. Reporters tied by tight deadlines have fewer opportunities to leave their offices and go out into the community. If the flow of reporter-originated copy declines, journalists may become more reliant on secondary sources of news fed to them by press releases and agencies.

Since the mid-1980s, the public relations (PR) industry has taken full advantage of the increasing pressure on mainstream journalism. Press and public relations officers are now usually the first port of call for a journalist seeking an official quote from sources which, at one time, were directly accessible to reporters.

Most institutions, both public and private, now have press officers, who act as mediators between journalists and management. They also promote their organisations, distributing press or media releases written in a style and tone that can easily be mistaken for journalists' copy. The text is ostensibly neutral but in reality is shaped to suit the interests of their (mostly corporate) clientele. Surveys show that PR accounts for 40–70% of what appears as news in the media.

Conclusion

The news-making process is dynamic and is shifting in response to changes in audience expectations and the commercial pressures of news production. Recently, we have witnessed a blurring of the boundaries between news and features, with celebrity exposés and sports personalities making the front page as often as stories about governments and conflicts. The news industry is, first and foremost, a business that has to respond to the demands of both its audience and its advertisers. It is employing ever-more editorially sophisticated and subtle means to maintain its market position. At a time of uncertainty for the commercial stability of advertiser-funded journalism, the news industry has also been forced to embrace major technological changes. Journalists must work on several platforms, when previously they might have worked on just one. Newsrooms and traditional journalistic roles are being drastically revised and re-organised. In this increasingly competitive and uncertain environment, the main question is whether a commercial model for journalism can deliver journalism that is in the public interest.

3
Global news for local audiences

Journalism, whether it comes to us through the Internet, radio, television or newspapers, can inform our ideas, values and beliefs and shape our understanding of the world. Effective media, that express diverse ideas, are essential to a properly-functioning democracy; people depend on reliable news and information to make informed decisions and hold their governments answerable for their actions. Likewise, now that large national and transnational businesses wield considerable political influence and economic power, effective media are vital for holding them to account. This particularly applies to the media companies themselves, who are often part of large, and increasingly transnational, corporations.

Given the vital role of the media in democracy, diverse ownership is important in ensuring that a small number of owners do not have undue political influence, limit the agenda for public discussion or suppress minority or alternative views. In its 1949 report, the first British Royal Commission on the Press reinforced the notion that the media industry is more than just a business; it also serves the public interest by informing readers about the issues that affect them. 'The democratic form of society demands of its members an active and intelligent participation in the affairs of their community, whether local or national.' The difficulty lies in achieving a balance between a free press, unfettered by governmental constraints and public subsidy and a vibrant, sustainable commercial press.

Around the globe, the media and technology landscape is being reorganized so rapidly that many are becoming deeply concerned that media production and distribution is being concentrated into the hands of a few, highly-interconnected, corporations, with possible consequences for diversity of opinion and content, creativity, competition and democratic access. This chapter will examine whether who owns what – and, more importantly, how much of it – has implications for journalism and society. Moreover, it will ask whether large corporations *should* control vast swathes of news and information.

Not so long ago, much local news was produced by and for the immediate community and, until the 1980s, media companies generally operated in a single nation. In the latter part of the twentieth century, increasing globalisation of the economic system coincided with technological developments and pressure to de-regulate the media to create ideal conditions for the development of global media conglomerates. While some small media organisations remain, most 'local' news is now produced outside the area it purports to cover and media companies have become so large they are now commonly termed 'media institutions'. 'Institution' connotes weight, influence and power: think of other familiar institutions, such as 'the Church' or 'the Family'. Because of this institutional context, concern is centred on journalism's interconnectedness with big business and specifically on the fact that the rules on who can own what have been relaxed. What worries critics the most is the trend towards the concentration, or consolidation, of media ownership into fewer and fewer hands; a significant number of outlets are now owned by a comparatively small number of corporations. In the UK, four major companies dominate the newspaper sector. In turn, some of those corporations are part of larger conglomerates. Several corporations have a cross-media presence, controlling film, television, music production and their distribution channels.

And in an increasingly competitive media climate, as news outlets vie for the diminishing amount of advertiser revenue, many media organisations are urging their governments to relax further the rules on media mergers and take-overs, in an attempt to reduce costs. They argue that a vibrant, flourishing commercial media is vital to ensure independence, choice and journalistic rigour. A market-led news business, they allege, will ensure that the audience's demands are met. But will it? And what will be the cost to journalism and society when a few major conglomerates control the dissemination of information?

Audiences, anti-censorship campaigners, politicians and journalists themselves worry both that media proprietors may have political motives and that business imperatives will override journalistic rigour. The news media are accused of political intervention, bias and distortion, lack of diversity, sensationalism and paucity of innovation. These issues are not new; they can be traced back to the vigorous control wielded by individual newspaper proprietors in the late nineteenth century. Looking back can help us see why present-day critics of concentrated ownership campaign for tighter legislation.

From political press barons to media proprietors

In the classic 1941 film, *Citizen Kane*, Orson Welles (who also directed) plays the eponymous newspaper owner, believed to be loosely based on the legendary media mogul, William Randolph Hearst. Welles's forbidding cinematography heightens Kane's Herculean omnipresence and through the film, we witness the power and widespread pressure that a media proprietor can wield. Kane's megalomania extends far beyond influencing his editor's front-page headline vocabulary; he controls the entire content of his title and uses his prominent position to enter the political arena. Of course, Hollywood cinema heightens emotion and exaggerates characters. Yet *Kane*'s enduring message – that those in control of the news have considerable influence at their disposal – has undoubted parallels in real-world journalism.

Media owners are often called 'tycoons' or 'press barons'. Whatever the appellation, they either control a media outlet through personal ownership or have a prominent position within the controlling company. The term 'press baron' is commonly associated with the nineteenth-century British proprietors, the Lords Northcliffe, Rothermere and Beaverbrook (each was raised to the peerage). The rise of the 'tycoon' coincided with the shift towards mass production of newspapers in the nineteenth century. In the USA, Hearst used populist – some would say sensationalist – journalism to draw mass audiences who had previously been deterred by newspapers' éliteness. Proprietors' influence did not go unnoticed by governments. Alfred Harmsworth (Lord Northcliffe) and his brother, Harold (Viscount Rothermere) founded the UK's *Daily Mail* and *Daily Mirror*. They ran the titles along the same populist lines as the burgeoning press in the USA: Northcliffe did not hesitate to use them for campaigns on subjects ranging from the benefits of the motor car to the benefits of wholemeal bread. However, his attacks on Government in the run-up to World War One set in motion several attempts to draw him into Parliament: an effort, he claimed, to repress his objections. He declined for several years but eventually took charge of the propaganda dropped behind enemy lines. His contemporary William Maxwell Aitken (Lord Beaverbrook), who founded the *Daily* and *Sunday Express*, was also drawn into the Cabinet and given a peerage by David Lloyd George.

Because they controlled newspapers read by millions of readers, Northcliffe, Beaverbrook and Rothermere felt fully justified in using their editorial powers to directly further their political aspirations. Notoriously, just before the 1924 general election, Rothermere's *Daily Mail* gave huge prominence to the 'Zinoviev letter'. The publication of this letter, it was claimed, was instrumental in securing the Conservative Party's victory. Though it is now thought to be a forgery, the letter was said to have been written by Grigori Zinoviev, head of the Communist International, to British left-wing activists, and was an attempt to discredit the Labour Party. But the press barons' campaigns were not confined to attacking the Left: Beaverbrook and Rothermere regularly criticised Stanley Baldwin, the Conservative Party leader, and sought to undermine his leadership by putting up opponents against Conservative party candidates in crucial by-elections. This fuelled a famous speech in which Baldwin condemned the press barons as 'exercising the prerogative of the harlot through the ages: power without responsibility'.

Although by the mid-twentieth century the era of the all-powerful, singular press baron was over, concerns about the concentration of media ownership in the hands of powerful people with potential political influence remained. The press enthusiastically continued its attempts to influence political parties and to direct readers in certain political directions. Hugh Cudlipp, the editorial director of the Mirror Group, believed that the *Mirror*'s 1945 'Vote for Him' campaign was responsible for turning a 'very comfortable Labour victory into a Labour landslide'. He was similarly convinced that the paper's efforts in 1964 made the difference between success and victory for the Labour Party.

In the latter part of the twentieth century, proprietorship expanded to include ownership of radio and television networks, film studios, publishing houses and Internet and other forms of multimedia companies. 'Press' barons became 'media' barons: some of the most prominent include Rupert Murdoch, Robert Maxwell, Conrad Black, Silvio Berlusconi, Axel Springer and Ted Turner.

THE *MIRROR*, MAXWELL AND MONTGOMERY

After several attempts, Robert Maxwell acquired the UK's long-established Mirror Group Newspapers in 1984. This self-made millionaire and Labour politician asserted a megalomaniac control over his titles that approached that of his press baron forebears. His authoritarian approach and desire for political influence was further shadowed when his business tactics came to light after he had gone overboard from his private yacht in 1991 in mysterious circumstances. It was discovered that he had stripped his employees' pension scheme of funding.

While Maxwell was something of a throwback, his successor David Montgomery is a classic example of the contemporary corporate newspaper proprietor. Montgomery, a former journalist, took over as chief executive of MGN as part of a package to rescue the group's titles. He cut costs, especially staff costs, ruthlessly but maintained his flagship newspaper's popularity. However, in 1999, he sought bidders for the group and it was taken over by the UK's largest regional newspaper company, Trinity, and renamed Trinity Mirror.

In the twenty-first century, locally- or nationally-owned media have been subsumed into huge global corporations. At the time of writing, nine major business entities – mainly US-owned – dominate the global media. For these corporations, journalism is just one part of a portfolio of media interests spanning production, distribution and, importantly, cross-promotion of their products. Newspapers and magazines owned by a company can be used to highlight its film and television output. Generating information, not just delivering it, is a growing business around the globe. In the United States, the communications industry is the largest private sector employer and the news media make up its largest segment. But in the whole of this vast country, most people get their news and information from just eight companies: Disney, AOL–Time Warner, Viacom, General Electric, News Corporation, Yahoo!, Microsoft and Google. The latter three companies are new starters, compared with the other five 'traditional' players, but their presence demonstrates that the Internet is becoming dominated by key players in the same way as traditional media formats.

SILVIO BERLUSCONI

Silvio Berlusconi is alleged to have used his almost total control of Italian commercial television to make himself Prime Minister of his country. Berlusconi, one of Italy's richest men (the US business publication *Forbes* estimated his worth at $9.4bn (€5.9bn)) created his fortune through a business empire, Fininvest, which spans media, advertising, insurance, food and construction. He also owns Italy's most successful football club, AC Milan. His business prowess has earned him many admirers, who feel his success qualifies him to run the country's affairs. Controversy has never been far away; he has faced many allegations of corruption and his involvement in every part of Italian life has angered critics, who say he has benefited heavily from favourable media coverage.

His company controls Italy's three biggest private television stations, while his associates run three public ones. Opponents complain that an Italian voter cannot escape coverage favourable to Mr Berlusconi. His extensive control over the media has been widely censured by both press analysts and press freedom organisations, who allege Italy's media has limited freedom of expression. Reporters Without Borders stated that in 2004, 'The conflict of interests involving Prime Minister Silvio Berlusconi and his vast media empire was still not resolved and continued to threaten news diversity'.

In the US, almost all journalism is regional, due to the sheer size of the country; for logistical, as much as cultural reasons, a dominant national press like that of the UK has not emerged. None the less, a strong corporate approach exists: large groups, such as McLatchy Company, Hollinger, Newhouse Newspapers and Tribune Publishing have bought much regional media and few independent local and regional titles now survive. The picture is similar in the UK; a few corporations dominate output in the print, broadcast and online sector both nationally and locally. Newsrooms once kept under the auspices of an individual proprietor who, for good or bad, created the paper's editorial strategy and identity, now work for faceless boards of directors. The top five regional newspaper publishers in the UK

RUPERT MURDOCH

Rupert Murdoch is unique: he himself is a far better-known figure than the global media conglomerate he runs. In recent years, Murdoch has become one of the most controversial media barons, frequently accused of abusing his power to support politicians such as Ronald Reagan, Margaret Thatcher, John Howard and George W. Bush.

Murdoch is chairman and chief executive of News Corp, which he founded in 1980 and is now the world's largest media conglomerate. News Corp owns more than 175 titles on three continents, publishes 40 million papers a week and dominates the newspaper markets in Britain, Australia and New Zealand.

The Australian-born Murdoch brought the expertise gained in his auspicious newspaper publishing career in Australia to a global market. Inspired by Northcliffe's populist style, his many acquisitions, alongside his papers' brand of high-profile campaigning tabloid reporting have brought him commercial success.

In 1986, Murdoch fought the powerful print unions working at News Corps' UK subsidiary, News International, when he intro-

RUPERT MURDOCH (*cont.*)

duced computer technology to automate production processes previously carried out by print workers. He moved production of his British newspaper titles – the *Sun*, the *News of the World*, the *Times* and *Sunday Times* – to Wapping, then a run-down area of East London and cut more than 5,000 jobs in the process. Today, Murdoch's global empire includes the Fox film and television studios, production, merchandise and broadcasting, book publishing, cable television networks, satellite broadcasting and a large portfolio of magazines, newspapers and multimedia interests. He owns some of the world's most influential newspapers, including the *New York Times* and the *Wall Street Journal*.

Murdoch's acquisitions have given him, as the major shareholder, an immense ability to promote his corporation's own output. In October 1999, *Time* magazine remarked that 'Rupert Murdoch is the first press baron to be a monster of the entire world. That's globalization for you'. But his power extends far beyond promoting BSkyB programmes in the *Sun*: his promotion of conservative views through his news outlets has attracted much criticism.

In Britain, Murdoch formed a close alliance with the Prime Minister, Margaret Thatcher, in the 1980s. The *Sun* credited itself with helping John Major win an unexpected election victory in the 1992 general election. However, Murdoch's switch to Labour, under Tony Blair, led some critics to argue that Murdoch simply backed the most likely candidate in the hope of influencing government decisions that might have affected his businesses. During the build-up to the 2003 invasion of Iraq, the editorials of all 175 Murdoch-owned newspapers world-wide were in favour of the war and the News Corp-owned *Fox News* was criticised over allegations of a pro-war bias before and during the invasion.

Today, in the UK alone, Murdoch's company delivers 35% of the national titles sold. More than half of the 76 million national newspapers sold each week in Britain come from just two publishers – Murdoch's News International and Lord Rothermere's Associated Newspapers.

in 2008 were (in order of weekly circulation), Trinity Mirror, Associated Newspapers, Johnston Press, Newsquest Media and Northcliffe Media. Newsquest is in turn owned by a US publishing giant, Gannett, which encourages its UK-based editors to take a ruthless approach to management. These five companies sold 48.8 million papers in a total circulation of 63.6 million in the regional and local sector.

Despite the commercial advantages major corporations have over small companies, even the biggest have been suffering a significant drop in revenue from advertising and a number of leading companies are urging governments to further relax rules on monopolies. When one business or company monopolises a sector and squeezes out all competition, consumers are left without a free choice. Governments have instituted legislation to prevent monopolies but media organisations say their industry is unlike others with the potential for monopoly, such as pharmaceuticals or fuel, and claim that further consolidation may be the only way they can survive.

In the US, Australia and elsewhere, media regulators have relaxed ownership rules preventing firms from controlling both a television channel and a newspaper in the largest cities. In the US, the Federal Communications Commission scrapped a rule preventing dual ownership of print and broadcast outlets in twenty cities. This decision overturned regulations that had been in place since 1975 and were specifically designed to support diversity of opinion and competition among news suppliers. Proponents of reform argued that the proliferation of cable television channels and the growth of the Internet meant such safeguards were obsolete but opponents argued that while the number of media outlets had exploded, the amount of different news providers had not risen. In the UK, the Competition Commission is responsible for scrutinising potential monopolies while the broadcast media regulator, Ofcom, takes on the task of ensuring editorial standards are maintained. In 2008, Ofcom controversially agreed to lighten the public service remit of regional stations, allowing them to cut back on local news and current affairs programming to maintain competitiveness.

When only a few players control media output, there will inevitably be a lack of choice and diversity for the audience and a greater potential for one-sided views. While economies of scale may permit major corporations to launch new titles or programmes, they will probably be produced by a smaller pool of staff, all using the same sources and adhering to the same overall editorial vision. Two pieces of evidence indicate that the corporate media environment may lead to a reduction in diversity: the recent professionalisation of the training and recruitment of new journalists and the decline in choice of outlets for consumers.

Traditionally, journalism has been viewed as a trade, a simple, unpretentious occupation, in which members trained through apprenticeship. Biographies of esteemed reporters frequently describe joining their local paper as an editorial assistant and honing their craft under the close and often stern scrutiny of the news editor. Few of these journalists could ever have imagined that their successors would start as reporters after just four years of higher education, like doctors or lawyers, yet it is now unusual for new recruits to enter without a university degree or some pre-entry training (and they frequently have both). A new entrant must go to a job interview armed with a battery of skills, often gained at their own expense – a sharp contrast to the traditional training route of on-the-job learning, indentures and a graduation from trainee, to junior then to senior roles. It is possible for a university graduate or postgraduate to get their first job in a national news outlet through having a qualification in media law or desktop publishing skills, whereas at one time it would take many years to reach this pinnacle. The identity of the journalist is morphing from intrepid outsider to rather more corporate, mainstream figure.

It has been argued that this change breaks the stranglehold that traditional indentures and training were perceived to hold on a recruit's progression. Today, raw talent and tenacity, ideally backed by a university education, spur promotion. However, university-level training must be funded by the undergraduate and sponsorship opportunities are limited. A postgraduate qualification in journalism is even becoming the preferred qualification, and often a stipulation, in job adverts and graduate traineeships. The cost of fees and living expenses can be prohibitive and mean students are much more likely to come from the middle-classes. But in becoming a middle-class profession, journalism might be losing touch with the views, opinions and experiences of vast swathes of the general public that it is meant to reflect.

The UK-based charity, the Sutton Trust, reported that leading news and current affairs journalists – so central in shaping public opinion and national debate – are more likely than not to have been educated privately. In the UK, independent schools educate just 7% of the population. Of the top 100 journalists in 2006, 54% were independently-educated; up from 49% in

SHARED NEWS PROVISION

Clear Channel Communications owns more than 1,100 radio stations across the USA, including all six radio stations in the city of Minot in North Dakota. There, in 2002, a train carrying a toxic chemical came off the rails and released a cloud of suffocating anhydrous ammonium fertilizer. The emergency services asked the newsrooms at the local radio stations to put out an emergency warning to residents. However, the Clear Channel local newsrooms were no longer staffed by journalists overnight. Instead, the radio bulletins were provided automatically from Clear Channel's syndicated news service in Texas.

1986. 'Not only does this say something about the state of our education system', said the Sutton Trust, 'but it also raises questions about the nature of the media's relationship with society: is it healthy that those who are most influential in determining and interpreting the news agenda have educational backgrounds that are so different to the vast majority of the population?'

New journalists are entering an environment where there is less choice for the audience. In many parts of the world, one major company may have total control over local or regional news outlets. One of the ways they can cut costs is to share news output across several titles or stations. But what might make business sense can result in a poor public service. The business imperative of the journalistic media, often manifest as seeking to maximise returns through advertising, might be seen as at odds with the public interest. Would an editor run a story that criticises a major sponsor? Might loyalty to an advertiser prejudice the journalistic integrity of the publication or programme? Most journalists would strongly refute any such suggestions. However, some argue that journalism rarely questions the benefits of business and capitalism in order to ensure the right conditions for furthering the corporate profit-oriented mission. By directing the context in which they operate, the news media are not simply a window on the world but an active agent in the story.

If companies dominating journalistic output suppress stories that are in the public interest, the public are denied information that the media, as the eyes and ears of the public, have a responsibility to deliver. On the other hand, media companies favouring relaxation of the rules on ownership argue that a commercial news organisation is far more likely to apply objectivity and newsworthiness as the principal standards of news judgement.

FOX NEWS AND MONSANTO

Journalistic principle was put to the test in 1997, when reporters Jane Akre and Steve Wilson produced a story on Monsanto's bovine growth hormone (BGH) for a Fox-owned television station in Tampa, Florida.

Akre and Wilson made a four-part series, in which they reported that BGH, which increases cows' milk production and had entered much of America's milk supply, was a risk factor in human breast and colon cancer. Just before the first programme was due to be aired, Fox received a writ from Monsanto's lawyers, alleging the programme's data were unscientific and biased and could not be broadcast. The journalists claimed they were told by their station's senior staff to change the story or lose their jobs.

Monsanto apparently put huge legal pressure on Fox to spike the investigation. Monsanto's advertising contract was handled by Actmedia, also owned by Murdoch. Wilson and Akre refused to remove the cancer allegations from the story and were fired. Akre sued the station under the Whistleblower Act. She won, but in February 2003, a Florida Court of Appeal overturned the decision, ruling that it was not illegal for a television station to distort the news. Nevertheless, the journalists have received numerous awards for their reporting, some of which has been aired online by their supporters.

Are de-regulated news media more independent?

There are many powerful arguments for allowing the media the freedom to exploit business takeovers and mergers and the journalism industry is at pains to defend its independence from any form of state control. A free commercial press, unfettered by public restraint, might deliver a more progressive, socially-responsible private enterprise. In this view, the media simply deliver what interests the public in exactly the same way as other producers and deliverers of commodities. The 'public interest defence' is that news and entertainment that has broad, mainstream appeal, attracts and retains advertisers and sells products is valuable and should be allowed to flourish; everything else is 'narrow and highbrow', the prerogative of an élite who seek to impose its preferences on fellow citizens.

Giant media corporations, some argue, have a greater chance of competing against other global organisations, possibly non-media based, which might seek to take over their assets and carry out even more ruthless cost-cutting. Moreover, without large media organisations there would be fewer media outlets because profits from successful parts of the businesses subsidise other, less-profitable areas, typically the news outlets. When a large media organisation takes over a smaller one, cuts are almost inevitable. Journalists and production teams find themselves working for several titles or programmes when they might previously have worked for one. This pooling of resources does not necessarily mean a drop in editorial standards: efficiencies can mean more money is available to invest in quality journalism. A large corporation with strong financial resources might be able to cater for diverse readerships, because a commercial company relies on continually satisfying its audience to secure advertising revenue.

Owners of major media companies contend that media regulation is a relic of the past, which hinders the 'old' media in adapting to a dynamic media landscape. Large corporations insist the relaxation of cross–media ownership restrictions will help deliver better-quality news and public affairs, and a more vibrant journalistic landscape will allow major players to change market positions frequently. This argument is demonstrated strongly in the business and professional sector of the magazine industry, where large companies can afford to close one title and launch a replacement that fits the market better. They see this as demonstrating a strong, competitive market that serves the public interest.

Supporters of greater de-regulation point out that until the mid-1980s, television had many fewer programming choices but today there are myriad specialist 24-hour news channels, financial channels, sports channels, shopping channels, men's channels, ethnic-programming channels and more. Cable and satellite channels offer documentaries, often produced by independent and freelance companies who might otherwise not have a market. This runs counter to the idea that diversity is fostered by more smaller media entities and that they produce better-quality news and public affairs programmes. A de-regulated media, with greater resources available to it, has more chance of delivering to a diverse audience. Instead of catering for one mass public, a larger corporation can visualise a range of markets, for many publics and is more able to take risks to reach uncharted niche audiences. The newspaper industry contends that relaxing the rules about one company taking over other media interests could stem the decline of print and increase diversity, arguing that economies of scale from cross-sector news production will increase resources for innovation; more topics and subjects will be covered, tailored to individual needs and interests. The notion that small local owners are inherently more objective than large corporations is equally contentious. Historically, some of the most biased outlets were locally owned and, being free of the scrutiny of shareholders or boards of executives, local owners are more likely than corporate owners to have ties to local political and business establishments.

Arguments for ownership deregulation favour mergers and acquisitions, because they play an important role in the evolution of the media. Mergers are a defensive strategy, which achieve economies of scale, capable of meeting the demands of modern media consumers and responding to competition from new outlets and technologies. Scale and scope are needed to provide information and entertainment at a reasonable cost; small outlets are not able to meet the costs of providing, for example, international coverage.

Ultimately, for supporters of deregulation, the plethora of new media forms makes the question of who owns what irrelevant. In the new media environment, they argue, it is fundamentally too complicated to impose rules in such a diverse ecosystem. Furthermore, they contend, it is unfair specifically to target 'traditional' media owners (the 'two out of three rule' in which proprietors are not allowed to own newspapers, radio and television in the same licence area) whilst an upsurge in new media goes unchecked.

Conclusion

Despite the industry's assertions that the competitive market-place would enable journalism to be diverse and responsive to public demand, there have been few successful new entries into the media arena since the start of the twenty-first century, let alone a flourishing of radical alternatives. The economics of advertiser-supported news outlets has created barriers that make it almost impossible for small, independent outlets to succeed. In particular, the rise of the modern commercial media system has highlighted the severe contradiction between privately-owned journalism and the needs of a democratic society.

When there were numerous newspapers in a community and when barriers to starting new media companies were relatively low, as was the case for much of the nineteenth century, it may have been plausible to suggest that a commercial media worked for democracy. Then, it was less of a problem for newspapers to express an editorial view, because alternative views were available: it is quite another thing to make such a claim today, when all but the largest communities are lucky to have more than one newspaper or other outlet, albeit usually owned by chains or very wealthy and powerful individuals.

In this context, for journalism to be partisan, for it primarily to serve the interests of the owners and the advertisers, would cast severe doubt on its credibility.

4

'Like penguins round an ice-hole': the law and ethics of journalism

The figure of the journalist has always been mired in controversy. In the public imagination there is great mistrust of journalists. Shady misdealing, self-interest and covert deception characterise the images of the journalist in celluloid, on screen and in print. Their real-world counterparts have not always behaved any better. A series of scandals has rocked American journalism in recent years and in the UK, trust in journalists is ranked at an all-time low. The behaviour of journalists working in the popular end of the market receives the most vitriol. Stories that probe a public figure's private life are the bread-and-butter of tabloid reporting. The illicit affairs of politicians, drug-taking of sports stars and celebrities' excess are the mainstay of publications such as *Heat* and the *News of the World* in the UK and the *National Enquirer* in the US. However, the vast majority of journalism does not involve scoring sensational exclusives. Most editorial staffs operate regionally and locally, writing stories about everyday events and organisations: councils, courts and general officialdom. While the Sunday scandal sheets might make it look as though journalists take undue liberties and publish very sensitive information, most journalists would say that they carefully navigate legal and ethical waters and verify even the most mundane information.

Journalists in the West are pretty much free to go anywhere, do anything and write anything that an ordinary member of the public can. However, a stringent set of legal and ethical frameworks, which seek to balance the interests of the media and the other parties involved can limit their activities. The aim of regulation is to maintain an equilibrium between the public's right to know and not unduly infringing the rights of individuals or organisations. Journalism is regulated because of the perception that media content (and media operations) can significantly affect economies, social policies, political debate and, above all, people's lives. Regulation is a complex process of judging – legally or by other means – what are acceptable and unacceptable practices. At its most basic level, regulation happens inside the mind of a journalist who surmises: 'I couldn't possibly put this in my story'; at the other end, there is an interesting mixture of ethics, regulation and the law.

People who travel soon notice how news content varies from one country to another: one country has a fair amount of explicitly violent content within its television broadcasts, while in its neighbour, reporting even basic information about crime is prohibited. The same applies to political and sexual content. Some rules are clear wherever you live: for example, it is never acceptable to publish fiction as fact. Other regulations might be controversial or pose dilemmas: is it right to publish the names and addresses of convicted criminals, when this might expose innocent members of their family? When is it acceptable to interview children? Is invading someone's privacy ever appropriate? Often, such differences are the result of legally-binding government regulations aimed at achieving standards for their societies that are consistent with prevailing philosophies of their domestic media.

However, journalists strongly resist any attempt to restrain them. Worldwide, journalists are united in striving to uphold the consensus of their right to report on matters of public interest, unfettered by unnecessary intervention from proprietors or state. Thomas Jefferson said, some two hundred years ago, that if he had to choose between government without newspapers or newspapers without government, he 'should not hesitate a moment to prefer the latter'. This vision of how a democracy should work prompted the framers of the American constitution to make free expression the first amendment of the 'Bill of Rights'; that Congress cannot enact a law infringing free speech or a free press. That brief clause has been the beacon for and the shield of the American press for over two centuries. But it is not carved in stone: it is tested almost daily in the courts, on the streets and in the corridors of power.

FIRST AMENDMENT DEFENCE

The *Courier-Journal*, based in Louisville, Kentucky, won the right to be given a copy of the Kentucky State Police's sex-offender database under the First Amendment. The state police already posts information on sex offenders on a website but the newspaper had asked for the complete database to enable it to analyse details and perform a closer scrutiny of the information. A circuit court judge ruled, on May 15, 2009, that the state police must hand over the database under the state's open-records law. Judge Phillip Shepherd's ruling affirmed a statement from the Attorney General's office that the material is public record. The state police challenged the opinion in an appeal to the circuit court.

The law and ethics of journalism are, both in practice and theory, intertwined and mutually reinforcing. By working within consensual legal and ethical boundaries, journalists – and by extension the journalism industry – can be trusted to strike a balance between the public's right to know and the citizen's right to be protected from unfair or unjust coverage (such as breaching privacy, jeopardising a fair trial or misrepresenting.

Most people are familiar with the concept of 'in the public interest' which, under appropriate circumstances, is considered a suitable defence for certain journalistic practices, such as intrusion of privacy or covert filming. But there is no clear-cut definition of what 'public interest' really means. What is it? Who defines it and how often? It is not only an enigma for journalists; regulatory authorities, editorial staff, trade unions and even the legal profession can waver or diverge over its meaning and application in the real world. Public interest, as far as the media view it, involves matters held to affect a considerable number of people and not, in general, matters that people are merely interested in knowing about – although this is less clear-cut where the popular press is concerned. Journalists working in crime, politics, health and conflict might readily be seen to be working 'in the public interest' but what about exposing celebrities' misdemeanours? Is CCTV footage of a pop star snorting cocaine in a nightclub toilet in the public interest? This might be seen as journalism produced purely with the intention of entertaining or 'interesting the public' rather than as a matter of concern that affects many lives. But it could be argued that this star, who makes their money from the public and potentially is a role model for their fans, ought to be behaving legally. That is a defence used by tabloid journalists accused of overstepping the mark.

In 2002, the BBC carried out a survey of public attitudes to public interest. More than three-quarters of the respondents wanted coverage of issues which are likely to affect them, reflecting the perceived role of the media as sources of important information. Surveys of audiences and journalists suggest that it is too simple to think that there is just one public 'out there' who can be satisfied with a one-size-fits-all definition of public interest. Diverse communities, different publics and audiences set in dissimilar contexts co-exist, defined by faith, age, socio-economic status, education and more. Something may be 'in the public interest' for one section of the population, yet jar with another. Therefore, it is hard to reach a consensus on 'public interest', particularly when social attitudes shift. In the 1950s, it was possible to sue for defamation if the media accused you of being gay. Nowadays, very few in Western societies would view homosexuality as a slur. Such shifts in morals and values can make it hard to predict the outcome of hearings into ethical or legal breaches.

The question of who defines public interest is also perplexing. Who in society is most qualified to speak for the consensus? Journalists have vigorously resisted judicial attempts to decide what is 'the public interest', possibly due to the belief that judges can be élitist or 'out of touch' with the views of the ordinary person.

Government regulation

There are strong arguments that the state should oversee the activities of journalists via strong regulation or the law. Currently, most self-regulatory codes of conduct, such as those determined by trades unions or professional-interest groups, are voluntary and cannot be enforced. Furthermore, the sanctions these self-regulatory codes and bodies can impose are limited and may not be enough of a deterrent. The journalists who preside over these codes and bodies may not be impartial in their judgement: they may see things more from the perspective of their fellow journalists rather than through the eyes of those who claim they have been harmed by the practices of those journalists.

A fundamental problem in enforcing journalistic moral values through self-regulation is that journalists, unlike doctors and nurses, are not licensed. If a doctor or nurse were to commit a serious act of professional misconduct, they would be unable to continue to work, as their licence would be suspended. This is not the case for journalists. If they breach an ethical code, the means of reprimanding them are limited. No legal framework forces outlets to follow the decrees imposed by the regulatory body. Newspapers may publish corrections but they are not required to print them on the front page: such items are often buried deep inside the paper where they can hardly be seen. In the unlikely event that a journalist is dismissed for breaching a code, they can still be employed elsewhere. Legal sanctions, fines and imprisonment might act as a greater deterrent, according to those who prefer greater curbs: the law is intrinsically absolute and the punishments for breaking the law severe.

All journalists, whatever their medium, must have a strong and up-to-date knowledge of media law. Very few editors of smaller publications, websites and broadcasting organisations would risk recruiting a journalist who could not prove – more often than not through qualification – that they have a comprehensive understanding of the law as it affects the reporting and presentation of news, and larger companies run regular refresher courses for their editorial staff. Defending legal actions can be very difficult and punitively costly for news organisations and indeed, has caused some to close down. The UK-based magazine *Living Marxism* closed after it was sued for defamation by ITN and two of its reporters. In 1997, *Living Marxism* ran a story accusing ITN of sensationalism in showing footage of a skeletal man incarcerated in a Serbian detention camp in Bosnia. ITN won the action and the jury (the jury decides damages in the UK) awarded £375,000 in damages against the magazine.

This is significant not only for journalists but also for those depicted in the story and for society. While it is obvious that falling foul of media law is hazardous to journalists, it can also be very damaging for the public. Reputations can be damaged irrevocably and unjustly and people may be tarnished by accusations of crimes of which they later prove to be completely innocent. In 2008, in an out-of-court settlement, a British citizen, Robert Murat, was awarded £600,000 against several British newspapers after they had intimated that he probably had something to do with the disappearance of a missing three-year-old girl, Madeleine McCann. Police in Portugal, where the child had gone missing in 2007, originally made Murat an official suspect but later said he had no case to answer. However, Murat said his life had been made unliveable by the detailed, accusatory reporting of his private life.

The consensus of the legal system in most Western democracies embraces the concept of the journalist as an exposer of crime, corruption and hypocrisy. Journalists ensure they know their rights of access to relevant official information and the courts and how they can go about investigating the people and establishments that exercise power and influence in society. Pressure groups, whistleblowers and investigative journalists armed with a comprehensive understanding of the law urge that the media industry should not shy away from testing boundaries and questioning those who seek to curtail journalists' rights, for example judges who attempt to impose restrictions to prevent the disclosure of a defendant's identity. Some investigative journalists work with a lawyer and actively seek loopholes in the law, enabling them further to contest authority.

The law is a shifting, dynamic entity and keeping abreast of its changes takes some effort on the part of reporters and editors. Often, it is the most newly-trained reporters who have the greatest legal awareness. Journalism law manuals must be frequently updated. In many countries, the law is not written down in an easily-searched handbook that can be referred to when a new case arises. In other words, it is not 'codified'. Instead, a great deal of legal judgment, by judges, juries and editorial decision-makers, is made through consideration of the precedents set by earlier trials. In the UK, until the seventeenth century, the legal system was based largely on judge-made law

(law developed as judges made necessary decisions on the cases brought before them – known as 'common law' or case law). Nowadays, judges must not only look at judgments made in British trials, they also have to consider European Community regulations and judgments in the European Court of Human Rights. The situation in US case law is similar.

The legal constraints that journalists most frequently face concern defamation of an individual or company's reputation, prevention of a fair trial, breach of privacy and reproduction of another's work without permission. In 1637, an English writer, William Prynn, made the unfortunate mistake of writing a book criticising Henrietta Maria, wife of King Charles I. Brought before the Star Chamber, Prynn was found guilty of libel and sent to prison. As an added punishment, he had his ears chopped off. Had Prynn been living in modern-day Britain or America, he would have more than likely been free to publish his book – whether about the present monarch or a US president – without suffering such drastic consequences. Defamation is predominantly a civil offence on both sides of the Atlantic, decided by juries made up of members of the public rather than by officialdom directed by judges. None the less, it is still an area of the law that journalists fear, as the outcomes can be uncertain and the effects hugely damaging to their companies.

Defamation is defined as 'false or unjustified injury to someone's good reputation'. Defamation laws have traditionally encompassed two areas: libel and slander. 'Libel' describes a written or otherwise permanent form of defamation; 'slander' refers to spoken defamation. Some believe this means broadcasters cannot be sued but they certainly can: libel laws apply to any permanent form, which includes radio, television and the Internet. Neither does using the word 'alleged' provide automatic protection from a libel charge. The test is whether the expression is capable of being proven true or false. Falsely accusing an individual, either directly or by innuendo, can result in huge damages for the complainant. Every year hundreds of libel claims are brought against newspapers, magazines, radio and television stations and websites by current or former public officials, entertainers or business executives who feel they have been damaged by critical journalism, usually an accusation or suggestion that the person has engaged in unlawful, improper or questionable activities. Repeating a rumour or simply making a mistake is no defence. The journalist must prove that the information is accurate, whereas the complainant has only to demonstrate that the words had the 'potential' to harm.

Libel cases, which are usually part of civil (rather than criminal) law, may be heard by juries: it is the jury, rather than the judge, that decides whether a journalist has published or broadcast libellous information. It is also the jury, whose members have no legal expertise, that decides how much the libelled individual has suffered and what kind of monetary damages they are entitled to receive in compensation. Judges have written guidelines and precedents to help them measure, for example, the worth of a limb lost through industrial injury but the value of a reputation is very hard to calculate. There are vast gulfs in the damages awarded. In 2006, a jury in the US awarded damages of $11.3m for a defamatory Internet posting describing someone as a 'con artist'; an international top-selling musical artist was awarded millions over allegations of lurid sex parties, while in 1992, the actor William Roache, who plays Ken Barlow in the UK soap opera, Coronation Street, was awarded 60p for being called 'boring' by a tabloid newspaper (the actual award was £50,000 but he lost all but 60p of it in costs, as he had refused an out-of-court settlement).

Damages can be affected by the consensus on the activities of journalists at any given time. In the UK in the late 1990s, a time when the popular press faced government criticism of their exposés, juries awarded huge damages. The Tory minister in charge of monitoring press standards at that time, David Mellor, warned the media that they were 'drinking in the last-chance saloon' and faced more stringent legal curbs on their practices. Mellor himself had been subject to press scrutiny over his affair with a young woman who later revealed lurid details about their sex life. Cultural shifts also determine what the 'right-thinking' member of society judges to be defamatory. In the 1950s, the flamboyant pianist, Liberace, successfully sued over press innuendos that he was gay. In 1957, the *Daily Mirror* columnist, Cassandra, described Liberace as: 'a deadly, winking, sniggering, snuggling, chromium-plated, scent-impregnated, luminous, quivering, giggling, fruit-flavoured, mincing, ice-covered heap of mother love'. At that time, homosexuality was illegal, and prison sentences awaited those found guilty. Liberace successfully fought other lawsuits in the US. Ironically, after Liberace died in 1987, his long-time bodyguard, Scott Thorsen, sued for maintenance from Liberace's estate. Today, cultural acceptance has shifted so greatly that few would feel that doubts over an individual's sexual orientation would result in a damaged reputation, though a 2003 case won by Tom Cruise against a gay porn star who alleged they had had an affair suggests doubt remains about the feelings of judges and juries.

THE *SUN* V BRUCE GROBBELAAR

The media do occasionally succeed in reversing juries' verdicts. A series of stories in the *Sun* newspaper in 1994 accused the goalkeeper, Bruce Grobbelaar, of match fixing. It claimed that the 43-year-old Zimbabwean had accepted money while playing for Liverpool and Southampton and that it had secretly-recorded video evidence. Despite the *Sun's* evidence, in 1999 a High Court jury returned a unanimous verdict in Mr Grobbelaar's favour and he was awarded £85,000 in damages plus £500,000 costs. It was claimed that there was no proof that the goalkeeper actually let in

THE *SUN* V BRUCE GROBBELAAR (*cont.*)

any goals to fix the outcome of the games. Undeterred, the *Sun*'s reporter, John Troup, continued to gather evidence and, in 2001, the Appeal Court overturned the jury's verdict, describing it as a 'miscarriage of justice'. Grobbelaar was forced to hand back the £85,000 to the newspaper.

An even longer-running case was that of the disgraced Conservative politician and author Jeffrey Archer. In 2001, he was jailed for perjury for 14 years after he won a libel action against the *Daily Star* newspaper over allegations that he had slept with a prostitute. In 1987, a jury awarded him £500,000 in damages. But a further investigation by the *News of the World* found that Archer had made a friend provide a false alibi.

In the US, the Constitution guarantees freedom of the press through a clause in the First Amendment of the Bill of Rights. Despite this, the libel laws varied from state to state until 1964 when the Supreme Court issued a ruling that revolutionised libel law in the United States. This famous case, *New York Times Co. v. Sullivan* created a national rule that was closer to the freedom guarantees of the First Amendment. In its ruling, the Court decided that public officials could only sue successfully for libel if reporters or editors were guilty of 'actual malice' when publishing false statements. The retired Justice, William J. Brennan Jr, who wrote the *Sullivan* decision, defined malice as 'knowledge that the [published information] was false' or that it was published 'with reckless disregard of whether it was false or not'. In other words, public officials could no longer sue for libel simply by proving that something that had been broadcast or printed about them was false but would have to prove that a journalist had knowingly printed false information while making little, if any, attempt to distinguish truth from lies.

For private citizens in the US, the test for proving libel is not as difficult; they can simply show that a reporter has been negligent when publishing false information about them. Negligence, like malice, is a legal term, and generally means carelessness on the part of a reporter or editor. Because private individuals have more reason than public officials to be left alone by the media, American libel laws consider that they are entitled to more legal protection from false statements. Besides making distinctions between public and private figures, American courts have also ruled that various kinds of published information are generally immune from libel charges. For example, it is almost impossible for a writer to be found guilty of libel if the writing deals with opinion rather than fact. 'Under the First Amendment, there is no such thing as a false idea', the Supreme Court said in a 1974 libel ruling. If the owner of a restaurant attempted to sue a food critic for a poor review of his establishment, they would more than likely be refused a hearing. This is the defence of 'fair comment' (which applies also in the UK). Fair comment is the 'common law defence that guarantees the freedom of the press to express statements on matters of public interest, as long as the statements are not made with ill will, spite or with the intent to harm the complainant'.

The uncertainty over the outcome of libel suits, and the potential for huge damages, means that newsrooms may avoid running controversial stories, where it can be very difficult for journalists to prove a story is true, even when they are certain of the facts. There is no guarantee that a source will testify in support of a journalist, especially if the journalist had protected their identity. A fundamental principle of a free and fair press is that people feel safe in speaking to the media. Without this protection, whistleblowers and others with serious concerns about major institutions or individuals would be deterred.

The prohibitive level of damages and costs can also deter all but the wealthiest media from going to court: smaller newspapers and television stations find it difficult to afford such a cost. There is also little doubt that libel writs are largely the preserve of the well-off. In the UK, because libel comes under the civil code, ordinary citizens rarely qualify for legal aid to pay for the action. Libel is also a civil rather than a criminal offence in the United States and there too, the enormous size of monetary awards and penalties levied by the courts in recent years has had a 'chilling effect' on journalistic enterprise, according to many in the news industry. Despite this, some celebrities have also found it hard to bring a suit. In 2006, a judge in Los Angeles threw out Britney Spears's lawsuit against the celebrity magazine *US Weekly*, ruling the pop star could not be defamed by published rumours that she and her husband had made a sex tape and were worried about its release. 'The issue is whether it is defamatory to state that a husband and wife taped themselves engaging in consensual sex', Judge Cole wrote in the decision document. 'The backdrop against which this issue must be addressed is that the plaintiff has publicly portrayed herself in a sexual way in her performances, in published photographs and in a reality show.' It is easier for US-based celebrities to sue for defamation in the British courts than in their own country, as British libel laws are more favourable to claimants. For instance, in the UK claimants do not have to prove malice, as they do in America. The right to freedom of expression is enshrined in the US constitution; in the UK the right is more evenly balanced against the individual's right to their reputation. Kate Hudson, the actress, pursued proceedings against the *National Enquirer* (which publishes a British edition) in the British High Court, rather than in the US.

The law of contempt bans the media from publishing, broadcasting or posting online any comments or information that might jeopardise active legal proceedings, in particular criminal proceedings heard before juries. The fear is that a juror might hear or see something outside the courtroom that might sway them in deciding whether the accused person is innocent or guilty. The law affects journalists as soon as criminal proceedings become 'active': that is, as soon as someone is arrested or charged. Contempt of court is a criminal offence and carries serious penalties of an unlimited fine and/or imprisonment. A classic example of contempt in criminal law is the publication or broadcast, once proceedings are active, of the fact that a person charged with a criminal offence has a criminal record. Revealing this information creates a substantial risk that people who may subsequently be on the jury could be influenced in their consideration of the facts and in making their verdict. Once a person has been convicted or acquitted, proceedings cease to be active and there is much more scope for commenting on the proceedings or making comments about the person. When a defendant has been convicted, newspapers often print page after page of very prejudicial material that simply could not have been printed during the course of the trial. This can happen between the jury returning their verdict and the judge passing sentence: judges are felt to be above media persuasion.

There has been criticism that the media may be flouting the rules, particularly in relation to when proceedings are active. Editors have largely been protected by the fact that police and security officials want information to remain in the public sphere as long as possible, to encourage more witnesses to come forward. It is argued that by the time a case is strong enough to take to trial, most potential jurors will have forgotten what they read at the time of arrest, even apparently damning evidence. This has opened a space in which newspapers in particular take greater risks, largely unchecked. On August 10, 2003, twenty-three British Muslims were held in police raids over 'alleged terror plots'. While the crimes were still 'alleged', the media concentrated on unambiguous headlines such as 'plot to blow up nine jets foiled', not to mention statements by the Home Secretary and the Deputy Commissioner of the Metropolitan Police such as 'we have stopped an attempt to commit mass murder on an unimaginable scale'. Much information that could potentially be regarded as highly prejudicial was published. Photographs of the accused were carried in newspapers, under the misapprehension that identity would not be at issue at trial. The media were leaked details of objects allegedly retrieved from the properties including cash, firearms and drugs. As proceedings were 'active', such reports were in contempt. The Attorney-General warned the press of the dangers (and was little heeded), yet no editors or journalists have been charged with contempt.

Invasion of privacy is one of the accusations most frequently made against journalism. Candid images of famous people on beaches or family outings daily fill magazines, newspapers and websites. The death of Diana, Princess of Wales, in a Paris underpass in 1997, whilst being pursued by the *paparazzi*, led to calls for curbs against over-zealous journalists. Editors argue that prominent figures must expect some interrogation of their personal life, especially when they are idols or role models to many and the news industry has fought vigorously against the introduction of privacy legislation.

On both sides of the Atlantic, the concept of 'privacy' has entered law only recently. Press freedom is a closely-guarded principle of journalism but it must be balanced by ensuring that people's private lives are not unduly subject to public scrutiny. Since October 2000, with the incorporation into UK law of the European Convention on Human Rights, people in the UK can act to enforce that right. Article 8 of the Human Rights Act includes a right to privacy and allows courts to grant an injunction (or 'interdict' in Scotland) to stop true stories about a complainant's private life being made public. The basis of the court's rulings is the balance of an individual's right to privacy against the media's right to freedom of expression (Article 10 of the Act). In the US, laws are geared less to protecting individuals from the intrusions of the press and more from intrusions by their government. The Privacy Act of 1974 (established after the Watergate revelations about the underhand actions of President Nixon) regulates government control of documents that concern a citizen. It gives citizens the right to see records about themselves, the right to amend them if they are inaccurate, irrelevant, untimely or incomplete and the right to sue the government for violations, such as allowing someone else to see certain documents without permission.

In journalism terms, copyright protects the legal owner of a story or image from having their work used without their permission. It is not permissible to lift a quote or information wholesale from another publication and use it as your own. At the very least, the source should be credited, if it is a small extract, or permission requested if it is a more significant amount. While there is no copyright in news itself, there is copyright in the words and images used to report it. Copyright may be owned by the outlet – often the case – or the journalists themselves, especially if they are freelance. It is indicated by the © symbol next to the name of the owner and costs nothing to assert. It is particularly easy to breach copyright rules in the use of photographs. There is some debate on whether a photographer who has been commissioned to capture images at a wedding owns the copyright for those pictures or whether it belongs to the couple who paid the bill. The photographer theoretically owns the copyright, so should freely be able to send the image for publication and self-promotion to a newspaper or magazine. But there is a 'moral right' clause in copyright law, which means the commissioner of the image, in this case the couple, has the right not to have the image publicly circulated. If the bridegroom's parents were to pass the image to the press without permission, both the couple and the photographer could justifiably complain that they had been wronged.

The Internet, once a somewhat unregulated media zone, is now subject to the same laws as print and broadcasting within the sites' host nations. This new and largely untested area of law has created a wealth of challenges and dilemmas for media outlets. The outcomes of breaches of laws guarding the Internet are hard to predict and few precedents exist. Inevitably, as new technologies come into use, and as societal expectations about media content react to them, the authority and jurisdiction of regulatory bodies is constantly being reorganised. One particularly fascinating area of technological change involves the convergence of traditional mass media with newer personal media. Traditionally, telephony and electronic media have been regulated by separate agencies. But the scale of delivery of online and multi-platform journalism from global media conglomerates to many different audiences, suggests a need to think about regulating all technologies by one agency.

Ultimately, even the most experienced journalists may find themselves 'sailing close to the wind' legally. Quite often they set sail deliberately, as a test of how far they can go. One journalist described a shift on a news desk during a major breaking story as like 'penguins round an ice hole'. By this, he meant that news organisations often follow the pack when it comes to, for example, naming someone arrested on murder charges. If one news organisation names a suspect without any repercussions, others will follow. If they are challenged, they cite the fact that as the name was already in the public domain, they were not making a new revelation. And they usually get away with it. Understandably, many believe that the boundaries of the law need firming, to control excessive behaviour by the media. However, journalists are united in their belief that tightening state controls on reporting is an affront to democracy.

There is a middle ground, in the form of the quasi-statutory bodies that regulate the broadcasting industry, though currently the print sector is entirely self-regulated. Ofcom in the UK, and the Federal Communications Commission (FCC) in the US, were founded in consequence of a legal process, resulting in a legal framework for their operations. The sanctions available to Ofcom are more far-reaching than those of the newspaper self-regulatory agencies. Ofcom holds the responsibility for issuing licences to commercial radio and television stations and there-fore also wields a significant weapon of reprimand: shortening or revoking those licences. In addition, Ofcom can impose fines. This power was exercised in 1999 by Ofcom's predecessor, the Independent Television Commission, when Med TV, a satellite television service for the Kurdish audience in the UK, made 'inflammatory' statements said to encourage acts of violence in Turkey. Ofcom is also involved in adjudicating complaints about the content of commercial radio and television.

WHEN JOURNALISM FALLS PREY TO PR

Berkshire-based 2-Ten FM radio station broadcast a news bulletin on 22 May 2008 that included an item about the risk of flooding to homes. The news presenter stated: '2-Ten FM's been told thousands of new homes in Berkshire are at risk of flooding because they're not being built with proper defences. A Reading flood protection company says developers are scared to put them in 'cos they're worried it'll put off potential buyers. Chris Phillips from Flood Defenders in Reading says extreme weather is something we're gonna have to get used to'. The news item then briefly featured Mr Phillips and the presenter concluded with: 'Check out photos of some of the high-tech ways you can protect your home [from flooding] online at 2tenfm.co.uk'. A listener complained that the report was 'sensational news hiding blatant advertising'. Ofcom was concerned about 'the apparent undue prominence given to products and services in the programme' and declared it a breach of its code.

In the United States, all broadcasters – public and private – are licensed by the FCC, an independent government agency. The FCC was established by the Communications Act of 1934 and is charged with regulating interstate and international communications by radio, television, wire, satellite and cable. The FCC's jurisdiction covers the 50 states, the District of Columbia and US possessions. In the early 2000s, the FCC began stepping up censorship and enforcement of indecency regulations, most notably following the Janet Jackson 'wardrobe malfunction' that occurred during the half-time show of Super Bowl XXXVIII. However, the FCC's regulatory domain with respect to indecency is restricted to the public airwaves, notably VHF and UHF television and AM/FM radio. Radio and television stations are licensed for eight years. Licence renewals are staggered across the country, so that they do not all come up for renewal at once. Licensing is used to ensure that both public and private broadcasters meet the public's 'interest, convenience and necessity' – a standard specified in the Communications Act 1934 that covers both media content and media accessibility. In a similar way to Ofcom in the UK, the FCC's approach to media content is the commercial marketplace. Both agencies respond to consumer complaints rather than actively regulate content before it goes on air. Like Ofcom, the FCC uses two main powers of enforcement to elicit compliance with regulations. The FCC's first power is to revoke a licence, or not renew it. The second, and main power, is to fine broadcasters that violate regulations or statutory law.

Self-regulation

Journalistic self-regulation involves media organisations uniting to establish voluntary editorial guidelines and ensure that they adhere to those rules. Self-regulation also entails providing a mechanism for complaints to be received and processed and some sort of sanction imposed if journalists breach the agreed guidelines. In this way the media, whilst remaining editorially independent of state control, acknowledge and administer their share of responsibility for the quality of journalistic practices and coverage within that nation.

An appointed, or selected, group of regulators – who may comprise a combination of senior journalists, interest groups and members of the public – work together to identify and enforce minimum standards with regard to accuracy, bias, representation and so on, while simultaneously allowing (in the case of newspapers), editorial freedom over what to report and what opinions to express. A process of adjudication ensures the media respond to legitimate complaints promptly, transparently and, where it is deemed necessary, correct mistakes. The most startling differences between the US, UK and the rest of Europe can be found in self-regulation. In Norway, the Netherlands and Sweden, for example, there is little formal regulation of the media. Instead, the journalists display a far stricter form of self-discipline, which lessens the need for legislation.

Self-regulation, both formal and informal, exists in individual media establishments (newspapers, radio stations, etc). Self-regulatory bodies are present on a grander scale in journalist's unions such as the National Union of Journalists (NUJ) in the UK, the Society of Professional Journalists in the US and the watchdogs, the Press Complaints Commission (PCC) and the Office of Communications (Ofcom) in the UK and the FCC in the US. These forms of regulation spring from the media industry's interest in keeping journalists in touch with public feeling and – far more importantly – keeping laws relatively unrestrictive.

An increasingly popular form of internal moderation is the news ombudsman, often known as the 'readers' editor'; a highly-visible person, brought in by the news organisation to improve public faith in their product. No two ombudsmen work exactly alike but typically they monitor news and feature columns, photography and other content for fairness, accuracy and balance in coverage. The news ombudsman receives and investigates complaints concerning published or broadcast news and feature material, often by obtaining explanations from editors and other staff members so they can respond to readers, viewers or listeners. He or she recommends appropriate remedies or responses to correct or clarify news reports. The ombudsmen are, of course, employed by the parent title but usually have direct access to the editor and other senior staff. They publish a daily list of corrections and a column on recent investigations and many write regular columns that deal with issues of broad public interest or with specific grievances. Where appropriate, these columns may criticise, explain or praise the outlet's editorial decision-making. By working with the organisation's staff, it is hoped ombudsmen can increase the awareness of editorial staff about the public's concerns.

In an oft-cited poll of jobs with integrity, journalism was near the bottom, alongside estate agents and traffic wardens. Despite many notable crusaders of responsible journalism, such as Carl Bernstein and Bob Woodward who broke the Watergate affair in 1972, the public view of the trade is, for the most part, quite damning and distrustful. Reporters are seen as shadowy figures, not to be trusted, who'd sell their granny for a scoop. Many journalists describe the look of horror on the faces of dinner party guests when their occupation is revealed: 'I'd better be careful what I say to you, then'. This is in sharp contrast to the way the industry and its employees view themselves; tenacious mediators, the eyes and ears of the public. If we conclude that it is impossible to restrict who can call themselves journalists, it becomes interesting to see how we make sure editorial output is confined to the realms of acceptability.

Getting the facts right should be journalists' most abiding priority. The news media have a responsibility to the public and to their sources to ensure that their coverage is reliable. Inaccuracies, even those which may seem minor, such as mis-spelling a name, can diminish public confidence in journalism if editorial staffs are not felt to be taking sufficient care. Journalists owe it to their audiences and to their trade to check facts metic-ulously. Factual errors can also deter important sources from working with the media in case they are misrepresented or misquoted. Accuracy is viewed as such an important principle in society that it is reinforced through the law of defamation.

Opinion and bias should always be kept out of news report-ing to ensure that readers and audiences are able to form their own judgments, based on factual information. Of course, polit-ical stories have to give a variety of viewpoints, so the audience knows where each party stands. But if the outlet is to retain credibility, the reporter should not take an editorial standpoint. Editorials and opinion pieces should be clearly separated from news pieces, as should advertising. Reporters face many tempta-tions, from free foreign travel to bribes, to prefer certain inter-ests. Some travel pages and websites would not survive financially unless tourism companies provided free transport and accommodation for reviewers. But it is very hard for individual journalists to remain credible if they are known to have personal or familial connections that might jeopardise their objectivity.

How journalists interact with and represent their sources is seen as essential to the public interest. Feeling confident about speaking to the media is vital for ensuring a vibrant, representa-tive public sphere. If individuals or groups feel they will not get access to journalists or fear their views might be distorted, the media are not reflecting their audiences' breadth of opinion. Anonymous sources tend to be frowned upon: editors are suspi-cious when a reporter files a story containing an innocuous but unattributed quote. Why will the source not stand by their words – are they inaccurate? There are circumstances in which a journalist may be justified in concealing the source's identity, such as when protecting a whistleblower. At one time in the UK, journalists were allowed to pay if securing the interview was in the public interest. 'Chequebook journalism' (the payment of sources for interviews) is widely used by the tabloid press to secure celebrity exposés and exclusives. Crime reporting can throw up dilemmas and much debate has occurred about paying victims and perpetrators of crime for interviews.

In 2001, the UK newspaper, the *Sun*, obtained the Great Train robber Ronnie Biggs's exclusive story and paid for a private jet to fly him back from exile in Brazil to the UK and to prison. Complaints were made to the Press Complaints Commission that this was in breach of Clause 16 of the PCC code, which prohibits payment to criminals except when it is in the public interest. The complaint followed a similar controversial case in 1998, when the convicted child killer Mary Bell was paid for her contribution to a book about her case. In Biggs's scenario, it was claimed that the *Sun* was using typical chequebook journalism to boost sales. On the contrary, argued the newspaper; it was performing a patriotic duty by bringing Biggs's back to justice after 35 years. The PCC did not uphold the complaints and wrote in its adjudication: ' To have censured the newspaper would have indicated that the actions of the newspaper were not in the public interest and that money was being channelled to Biggs in order, in some way, for him to benefit from his crimes. Neither argument was sustainable'. The US-based Society of Professional Journalists does not prohibit paying criminal sources but urges 'caution' when dealing with criminals, active cases and generally when paying for information. A more clear-cut ethical breach is the payment of witnesses who are taking part in active criminal trials where their evidence might have the potential to be distorted. This has been outlawed in several countries.

Other ethical difficulties are restricted in law, including the way children are reported, the probity of financial journalism and the use of intrusion and subterfuge as a means to obtaining information and discrimination. Children must not be identified if they are victims of sex crimes and it is appropriate to seek parents' or guardians' consent before interviewing and identifying minors. Journalists should not benefit from information about financial opportunities that reaches them before publication. This follows the conviction of two of the 'City Slicker' journalists who wrote a finance page for the UK *Mirror* newspaper and bought shares before writing about them. This was considered a serious breach of journalism ethics. The two were found guilty of misleading investors and share-tipping. The concepts of intrusion and subterfuge, where they breach someone's human rights, are now part of privacy laws. Journalists have ethical codes that apply to intrusion into grief and shock, which determine under what circumstances it is, for example, acceptable to contact the bereaved.

Going undercover or covert recording is usually only deemed ethically acceptable within the professional codes and the law if it is used as a very last resort, when other reporting techniques have failed to garner evidence. This is a response to the tendency for the journalistic research methods of some outlets to be deliberately dramatised, as a ratings booster or spectacle. Shaky footage from hand-held cameras may be very televisual but do the story and the 'public interest' warrant a breach of privacy? Could the information be collected in a simpler way that would minimise harm? Given the lengths that journalists may go to, there is an ongoing debate about whether self-regulation or state control is the best way to curb the excesses of certain practices.

Conclusion

There are strengths and weakness on both sides of the argument for and against tighter state-enforced controls on the media. A self-regulated media can fight more effectively for the repeal of unnecessary regulations, by convincing the public that the media are conscious of the need for standards. Effective self-regulation should maintain journalism's credibility to the public, whilst simultaneously protecting the right of journalists to be independent, as they are judged by their peers and the public rather than those in power. A robust self-regulation system lessens pressure on the judiciary system to sanction journalists, as complaints can be dealt with cheaply and swiftly, unlike court proceedings. Printed corrections and public – and voluntary – acknowledgment of mistakes are satisfying for the complainant. Ultimately, by minimising state interference in the media, self-regulation is better placed to promote democracy. That is the theory, anyway; the reality is different when self-regulatory bodies appear to have very little power to sanction erring journalists or provide adequate deterrents. The evidence is that a growing number of people who feel they have been wronged by the media are seeking recourse through the courts, circumventing self-regulatory bodies. A recommendation that a paper publishes an apology has been proven to be of little value as a deterrent or recompense for harm, and the regulatory bodies have not been active in warning the media that they are sailing close to the wind.

Three developments are possible: industry self-regulation has to be seen as more effective, the media may have to accept an external moderator who can ensure that adjudications are fair and just or legislation may have to be tightened. This last notion, while it might reduce the amount of scurrilous behaviour on the part of reporters, might also deter investigations into matters of public concern.

5

'We're all content providers now': journalism and technology

Citizen journalists, content providers, bloggers: many new job titles have entered the editorial lexicon since the 1990s. The Internet has wrought huge, fundamental changes to the practices and processes of journalism yet many commentators say we are only at the beginning of a digital 'revolution' in news production and dissemination. Rapid developments in technology are transforming the ways we receive news, by whom it is produced and how it is gathered and disseminated. Both in the media and in the wider society, many believe these changes have huge implications for the future of journalism, especially in terms of public trust and the standards of practice within the trade. As the craft is swept along at high speed on a journey for which it is not fully prepared, the future of journalism is in the here-and-now – multi-platform, multi-skilled and mired in doubt and controversy.

Technological developments in journalism have always aroused suspicion in its practitioners. When 24-hour rolling cable and satellite news was launched in the late 1980s, commentators warned that such instant access to news would kill off print journalism. Two decades later, although newspaper sales have been declining, the availability and accessibility of news has increased. More significantly, technology has gradually altered the balance of power between news provider and news consumer, challenging the authority, function and status of journalism. A new publishing model is emerging: control is shared and innovation is arising from partnership between news providers and their audiences. This is a very different model from the traditional, 'top-down' view of the journalist/ audience relationship, in which the news provider hands down to their readers, listeners and viewers what they feel is important.

One of the causes of alarm is the speed at which the new media technologies have taken centre-stage and transformed the journalistic landscape rapidly, radically – and often controversially – for all media. Boundaries between different formats have been flung open and news brands compete across formats. Radio news not only comes through the airwaves but has images and video on its accompanying website; readers browsing a newspaper website will find a video of that hour's headlines. The Internet is at the centre of newsrooms of world-wide broadcasters and local newspapers alike and journalists are profoundly changing the way they work.

The public growth of the Internet began in the 1990s, as increasing numbers of computers came into homes and workplaces. The simultaneous development of the text mark-up language, HTML, enabled the creation of attractive, user-friendly websites. The first online newspaper was published in the US, on the now-defunct 'videotext' service and the Chicago-based *Tribune* was among the first titles to put its content online, in 1991. As the decade progressed, software developments made the task of creating online content quicker and cheaper – between 1995 and 1998, the number of US dailies on the web grew from 175 to 750. Newspapers in the UK followed the same pattern: in 1994, the *Sunday Times* became the UK's first newspaper to have an online edition and a few months' later the *Daily Telegraph* launched the *Electronic Telegraph*, Europe's first online daily.

In August 2006, the UK National Office of Statistics' report *Internet Access: Household and Individuals* noted that a substantial 60% of the adult population regularly accessed the Internet. Most of those regular users were young, educated professionals – just the market that news organisations' advertisers were eagerly trying to engage with. It is not surprising that the news media were keen to tap into the opportunities the Internet offered. Even in public service broadcasting, there was 'no choice': the web was where young people were going, according to Bob Eggington, the BBC journalist in charge of the project. The BBC launched its news website in 1997, some four years after CNN had gone online.

Most major news providers, generally referred to as mainstream news sites, host websites that offer the same content as the print or broadcast media. Journalists who work for newspapers, particularly local and regional titles, first have their copy published to the web and then printed in the newspaper. These websites are cost-effective to produce and highly attractive to the 'netizens' who use the Internet as their first and regular news source. The advantage to major news brands is that they have an established and largely trusting audience who, the brands hope, will take that loyalty with them to the website. The advantage to the user is that the sites are free and regularly updated, and web archives mean it is possible to access a story days and even months after it was published.

Websites offer journalists the chance to be versatile. Far from being restricted simply to print, they can enhance their story by adding links to other sources and sites offering further information. Bigger news organisations can include links to related archive material. Traditional broadcast or print formats face constraints on how much airtime or space they can give to unfolding events, such as war or conflict. Such constraints dictate that the latest and most immediate information will be more newsworthy to editors than the context and history that may have led to the conflict. However, news websites – and especially their archives – allow the user to read into the story in greater depth. Furthermore, web archives remain accessible, whereas broadcast and print forms become harder to retrieve as time passes. Journalists working for good websites can thought-fully configure the way the information is organised and mediate the story for swifter and less ambiguous uptake, through careful design and layout and the incorporation of visual, audio and graphical elements. There is no doubt that in the decade or so that mainstream news sites have existed, they have harnessed the versatility and interactivity of online communication with increasing boldness.

News aggregators, such as Google News, newsnow.co.uk and some parts of ananova.co.uk, have developed in response to the vastness of the field of online news. An aggregator can provide either a searchable index of stories collated from innumerable sites world-wide or, as in the case of newsnow.co.uk, regularly update indexes of stories breaking on the web. Ananova.co.uk is something of a hybrid between mainstream news site and aggregator; it trawls the web for global stories and repackages them for UK audiences. Ananova also classifies stories according to genre, which makes it a popular source for other sites and media as well as a site in its own right. The quality and use of aggregators is highly-dependent on the number of sources they searched.

THE HUFFINGTON POST

The Huffington Post was launched in 2005 as the blog by socialite Arianna Huffington, who invited her influential friends to post commentary on political and social issues. She aimed to offer a liberal alternative to the conservative stance of dominant newspapers. Within two years, the *Post* was receiving huge numbers of

THE HUFFINGTON POST (*cont.*)

hits and its aim is now to be an alternative online newspaper, with international, national and local news and comment. President Barack Obama is one of the many high-profile people who have produced blogs for the site, which also hosts an area for ordinary citizens to post their own reports. Although it has received awards, the site has simultaneously attracted controversy, mainly for the strength of opinion expressed on its comment boards. None the less, with a staff of fewer than 60, its hit-rate rivals the established US online newspapers. Funded through donations and private equity funding, in 2008 it was estimated to be worth $100m. The site launched a campaign to recruit ten investigative journalists made redundant by the mainstream media to carry out inquiries into the state of the economy.

Blogging

Whereas news websites and aggregators conform largely to the model of news being produced by professional journalists for lay audiences, the development of weblogs has transformed the news consumer into news producer. Although most blogs reflect the views of one very partial creator, now, a range of blog types has developed from the basic concept of a personal form of serial online posting. The US-based blogger, Matt Drudge, was among the first to expose the Bill Clinton and Monica Lewinsky scandal in 1998. Some bloggers, such as the British political blogger, *Guido Fawkes*, overlap with the mainstream political media: Fawkes posted emails sent by the Labour spin–doctor Damian McBride describing his intention to deliberately and inaccurately smear leading Conservative ministers. Other blogs, such as *Media Matters for America*, act as watchdogs. While blogs add openness and critical debate to reporting, they have increased the amount of unverified information in the public domain. None the less, blogs give campaigners and the public the power to contribute to political discourse, blurring the line that once existed between journalism and activism and even beginning to affect political events.

HUMANISING POLITICS?

During the 2007 federal election campaign, hundreds of thousands of Australian voters watched footage of the opposition leader, Kevin Rudd, apparently eating his own ear wax, while the Prime Minister, John Howard, was portrayed as old-fashioned. Despite his *faux pas*, Rudd won the election, because the video changed people's opinions; voters saw his as less steely and more human.

Blogs have been joined by micro-blogs. *Twitter* is a free social networking and micro-blogging service in which users send and read 'tweets', text posts of up to 140 characters in length. Users can receive updates via the Twitter website, mobile phone, instant messaging, Short Messaging Service (SMS), Really Simple Syndication (RSS), email or through an application such as Facebook. We might question how useful a news tool a service limited to 140 characters can be but in July 2008, there were more than two million Twitter accounts world-wide and news organisations were using it live on air. While the technology is in its infancy, its journalistic supporters claim it has huge potential for discovering breaking stories and carrying out interviews: Twitter has been used to send questions to specific professional or social groups to elicit instant responses and to gather questions that the public would like put to those involved in a major news story. In 2008, CNN asked viewers to send in questions to their on-air financial experts about the global credit crisis and at the height of Hurricane Gustav in the same year, the CNN anchor Rick Sanchez read out Twitter tweets from viewers trapped in their homes. Because it is so quick and easy to use, bloggers find it a better way to relay information instantaneously than posting a full account online. Twitter has been used very effectively to relay live information from natural disasters. For example, the blogger Robert Scoble claimed to have reported a major earthquake in China over an hour before the news appeared on CNN, because he had seen Twitter posts from local people describing the tremors as they occurred. The phenomenon has been embraced by political leaders, as a way of keeping in contact with the electorate. The US presidential campaigns and the UK Prime Minister's Office use Twitter, as do political journalists and policy advisors, suggesting that it is already a tool for the media élite rather than computer 'geeks'.

The practices of blogging and micro-blogging raise questions. As with any form of indirect contact, how can the journalist verify who they are communicating with? It would be quite easy for someone to misrepresent themselves; something which is easier to detect in face-to-face and telephone interviews. But for instant polls and as one source among several for a story, they clearly have huge potential. It all comes back to the need for informed and experienced journalistic judgment; ensuring new technologies are used ethically, legally and in the public interest.

While blogging and micro-blogging are fundamentally text-based, albeit with the capacity to add other media, podcasting is a method of publishing and broadcasting audio online. Podcasting automates the process: once a user has subscribed to a podcast, new files are automatically sent to their computer via an RSS 'feed'. The user can listen to the shows when and where they want, either on an MP3 player or on a computer. Podcasting originated in America, where bloggers found it easier to get more words out through speaking than writing.

Traditional radio broadcasts make a natural transition to podcasts. (Although there are difficulties over rights of re-broadcasting music, so radio programme podcasts often cut it out.) The *Telegraph* claims to have been the first UK national newspaper to offer a daily news podcast, starting with columns read by its journalists. The paper later appointed the former BBC journalist Guy Ruddle as its podcast editor. The *Guardian's Media* section podcasts a weekly round-table discussion with senior media figures. Largely, the media are still exploring podcasting's possibilities. It has the potential to deliver tailor-made radio for niche groups, as opposed to a one-size-fits-all approach. And the ease with which citizen journalists can create podcasts and post them alongside mainstream news allows the public to intervene in journalistic discourse.

Computer-assisted reporting

Increasingly, journalists use new formats not just as media but as sources, turning to websites and social networking sites to search for information, case studies and images related to major breaking stories. Although perfectly legal, the practice has raised concerns about targeting vulnerable groups and gaining access to sensitive information. The massacre at Virginia Tech in 2007 brought home the ease with which journalists could use sites such as MySpace and Facebook to get witnesses' accounts and pictures of the perpetrator and his victims. The UK newspaper watchdog, the PCC, carried out a study into the public's attitudes about the media and social networking which found that 78% of people would change the information they publish about themselves online if they thought the material would later be reproduced in the mainstream media. The PCC found that only 55% of people consider, before posting information, that it might be used by journalists or employers without their consent.

Online, the distinction between private and public is increasingly blurred. Journalists have a responsibility to behave ethically but their challenge is in agreeing how this applies to personal data published online but not intended for the mass media.

At one time, if journalists wanted official data, they had to rely on information gathered by agencies such as government departments and presented to them second-hand. The danger was that the data had been manipulated, for example to present the provider in a positive light. Rather than relying on authority, reporters now routinely collect information in databases, analyse public records with spreadsheets and statistical programs, study political and demographic change with geographic information system mapping, conduct interviews by e-mail and research background for articles on the Web.

Computer-assisted reporting (CAR) is the term coined to describe this use of computers to gather and analyse data first-hand and specifically to create reports that challenge rather than confirm the official view. CAR has grown rapidly in recent years, as computers have come into everyday use, but its roots go back for decades. The first actual instance of computer-assisting reporting was in the 1952 USA presidential election, when CBS used a computer to predict the outcome of the race between Eisenhower and Stevenson. Professor Philip Meyer, of the University of North Carolina, is also credited as one of the innovators in computer-assisted reporting, for his coverage of the 1967 Detroit riots. He conducted a survey among African-Americans and revealed that, contrary to the contemporary hypothesis, people who had attended college were equally as likely to participate in riots as those who had dropped out of high school. The story won him a Pulitzer Prize. CAR techniques expanded from polling and surveying to a new opportunity for journalists: using the computer to analyse huge volumes of government records. Since the mid-1990s, programmes such as the National Institute for Computer-

Assisted Reporting (NICAR, created by the not-for-profit foundation, Investigative Reporters and Editors) have been used to promote and educate journalists in the use of CAR.

One type of CAR story that has become common in the United States is the surveillance of sex offenders listed on the public registers introduced since the mid-1990s under the 'Megan's Law' legislation. Newspapers and television stations across the United States have used mapping software to uncover sex offenders living closer to schools than local law allows. One concern, a response to the UK newspaper the *News of the World's* decision to print images of convicted paedophiles, is that journalists may be overstepping the boundaries of their responsibilities and acting as law enforcers. Following this newspaper's campaign, innocent people mistaken for paedophiles were subject to vigilante attacks and police and children's charities warned that real offenders might change their identities to avoid attack, thus evading police monitoring. However, it could be argued that the information might help to expose perceived deficiencies in the justice system, which is in the public interest. By surveying and analysing databases, reports and public records, CAR can help the media find exclusive stories by identifying trends and patterns in official data, be it hard news, such as crime statistics, or lifestyle issues, such as the 'luckiest' day of the year to get married. Supporters of CAR believe it will help maintain and improve the media's watchdog role.

Every new media format carries issues as well as opportunities for journalism. New technology can challenge the embedded routines by which news agendas are set up. Determining what events and topics make it on to the mainstream news agenda has typically been viewed as instinctive; honed through news desk experience rather than made by deliberate strategy. However, sociologists of news have shown that newsworthiness is less to do with instinct and more to do with values that become established and reinforced through newsroom routine.

The growth of digital technologies not only changes the relationship between traditionally separate media but also the relationship between news media and their audiences from stable, top-down and directed to dynamic, charged and constantly re-negotiated.

COMMUNITY ACTIVISM

In 2005, argument was rife between residents of Brighton, Sussex, UK, and their local council over proposals to introduce community 'wheelie bins'. Frustrated by a lack of coverage of the heated debate in the local press, residents started a dedicated website where the matter was debated articulately and thoroughly, involving both residents and key council officials. Jemima Kiss, of journalism.co.uk, reported: 'That's an example of micro-citizen journalism really but the issue needed thrashing out. It was free and quick to do online and local media should be asking themselves why they didn't provide an adequate platform for the debate'. (www.journalism.co.uk/2/articles/51458.php.)

By 10:15am on the morning of the London bombings, July 7, 2005, there were more than 1,300 blog posts about the blasts, according to the blog tracking service, Technorati. As mobile telephone lines were jammed and mainstream news services faced an information black-out in the incident's early stages, blogs were a significant source of information for many Londoners, as well as concerned relatives. While many blog posts expressed concern for people who might have been caught up in the explosions, others summarised and provided links to online news coverage. Some blogs took on a public-service journalistic function, hosting roll-calls of people who might normally be in London and posting safety advice from the police. Inevitably, speculation about the cause of the blasts started at an early stage.

GEORGE BUSH'S MILITARY SERVICE

In the lead-up to the 2004 US presidential election, Dan Rather, anchor of CBS News' *60 Minutes* programme broadcast a story about newly-discovered documents about President George Bush's military service between 1968 and 1974. The documents appeared to show that Bush, whose service in the Texas Air National Guard ensured that he did not have to fight in Vietnam, had hardly turned up for even basic duty. This was denied by the White House and conservative bloggers, who claimed that the report had been based on falsified documents. CBS retracted the story, saying that the documents' authenticity could not be verified. Rather, who had been with CBS for decades and was one of the most familiar faces in American journalism, was fired by the network the day after the 2004 election. He has since launched a $70m lawsuit against CBS and their parent company Viacom, claiming he had been made into a scapegoat.

There are still relatively few non-mainstream news blogs in the UK and even fewer, if any, have yet wrestled the agenda-setting and revelatory function from professional news-gatherers. More often than not, news blogs are linked to mainstream news websites. For example, the *Guardian Unlimited* site has a large 'Comment is Free' section, featuring blogs from its journalists of their personal reflections on the issues of the day. In the US, there have been claims that blogs have acted as a new political force in disclosing irregularities in, for instance, reporting by CBS News.

It is easy to be cynical, and suggest that the mainstream media are humouring their audiences by feigning blogging's (perhaps idealised) authenticity and independence. But the rise of blogging may have been more than superficial. The BBC's *Editor's Blog* often explicitly reflects on editorial judgments, suggesting an openness and transparency to the news-gathering and selection process that were previously concealed from audiences. The BBC's acclaimed business editor, Robert Peston's, blog is hugely influential in providing information about the credit crisis. Indeed, the speed with which he posted exclusive information about troubled financial institutions may have played a part in shaping government attempts to remedy the situation.

While the authority of the host news organisation may beckon the reader in, the user is encouraged actively to navigate the linked information. For example, on the blog area of telegraph.co.uk, a blog entitled *Parliament at its Worst,* posted by Daniel Hannan on January 21, 2008, about the European Treaty, carried a list of 'tags' beneath its headline including Europe, MPs, EU Referendum, EU Treaty, unpopular politicians. The piece was followed by a number of replies from readers. A BBC Online story about flooding in the north of England published on the same day, 'Floods cause road and rail chaos' (news.bbc.co.uk/1/hi/england/7200166.stm) contained links to the Environment Agency, Durham County Council and local weather and travel guides. There were also pictures sent in by the public and a direct invitation to readers to share their experiences. By stimulating the reader's sense of enquiry, mainstream blogs can represent a middle way between institutionalised journalism and the 'blogosphere'.

Widening access to previously untapped sources of news might be better achieved through other methods presently at the leading edge of new technology, for example through what blogger Jeff Jarvis terms 'networked journalism'. He writes:

> In networked journalism, the public can get involved in a story before it is reported, contributing facts, questions and suggestions. The journalists can rely on the public to help report the story; we'll see more and more of that, I trust. The journalists can and should link to other work on the same story, to source

NETWORKED JOURNALISM

The devastation wrought on Florida by Hurricane Katrina in 2005 prompted local media to explore networked journalism as a swift and influential means to provide powerful evidence of misman-agement of the clean-up operation. In May 2006, the Fort-Myers *News-Press* was contacted by readers complaining about high prices being charged to connect re-built homes to water and sewer pipes. In response, the paper called on readers to perform their own investigations, which resulted in analysis by engineers, accountants and even construction company whistleblowers. They did not just harness the support of local lay-investigators; they were supported by people from all over the world who had accessed the story online. The networked journalism exposed wrong-doing to the extent that officials resigned and changes were made to the handling of construction bids.

material and perhaps blog posts from the sources. After the story is published – online, in print, wherever – the public can continue to contribute corrections, questions, facts and perspec-tive … not to mention promotion via links. I hope this becomes a self-fulfilling prophecy as journalists realize that they are less the manufacturers of news than the moderators of conversations that get to the news.

www.buzzmachine.com/2006/07/05/
networked-journalism/

Hyperlocality

One of the key ways in which public participation in journalism can help is to ensure that coverage is universal, rather than origi-nating from where mainstream news organisations have placed reporters and bureaux. The term 'hyperlocal' is sometimes used to refer to news coverage of community-level events which the mainstream media would not previously have covered unless the story had mass appeal. It is significant that the idea of hyperlocal has strengthened at a time when many fear that the globalisation of media corporations threatens local coverage. In fact, mainstream media are embracing the hyperlocal to stem leaks in advertising revenue. The UK regional newspaper group, Trinity Mirror, set up several hyperlocal websites for user-generated content in 2007, the content of which went into a series of hyperlocal free-distribution newspapers. In the same year, The *Washington Post*, well known for its detailed coverage of White House and global affairs, introduced a site with news and other information for the people of Loudoun County, Virginia, which has a population of 272,000. The site features church schedules, restaurant menus and live high school football scores – things that normally would not make it into the pages of the *Washington Post*. Readers download content from the site on to their iPods, phones and even video-game consoles. They can click on a street address and see the closest events and news.

Hyperlocality does not necessarily have to be geographic; niche interest groups, from new mothers to vintage car enthusiasts, capitalise on the ease of starting a website. YouTube's news video section, *Citizen News*, launched a competition for user-generated content in September 2008, which they say will create a 'more diverse media dialogue'. Early postings include video of Sudanese attempts to improve the clean water supply to rural communities, stories from inside soldiers' barracks in Afghanistan and images submitted by ordinary people from the heart of Hurricane Gustav, which battered the southern states of the USA in 2008. In South Korea, *OhmyNews* became popular and commercially successful with the motto, 'Every Citizen is a Reporter'. Founded by Oh Yeon-ho on February 22, 2000, it has a staff of some forty traditional reporters and editors who write about twenty per cent of its content, with the rest coming from other freelance contributors who are mostly ordinary citizens. *OhmyNews* has an estimated 50,000 contributors and has been credited with transforming South Korea's conservative political environment. In 2001, *ThemeParkInsider.com* became the first online publication to win a major journalism award for a feature that was reported and written entirely by readers, earning an Online Journalism Award from the Online News Association and Columbia Graduate School of Journalism for its 'Accident Watch' section, where readers tracked injury accidents at theme parks and shared accident prevention information. During the 2004 U.S. presidential election, both the Democratic and Republican parties issued press credentials to citizen bloggers covering the convention, marking a new level of influence and credibility for non-traditional journalists.

While for many, the melding of journalism with interactive technology is seen as positive and as heralding a democratisation of 'top-down' news delivery, others fear journalistic standards are under threat. Instead of gaining access to ever-increasing quantities of originally-sourced and carefully-crafted news, are we on the brink of killing off journalism? Are we able to distinguish between facts and fiction when we are bombarded with conflicting information from mainstream and alternative news providers? It is perhaps unsurprising that most dissent and fear emanates from journalists. The Commission on Multimedia Working, established by the UK National Union of Journalists to investigate the implications of media convergence, has found widespread concern about the impact of new media working on journalistic standards. Their 2007 report, *Shaping the Future*, found that the significant sums that have been spent on new technology have not been matched by investment in the practice of journalism. Journalists working in new 'integrated' newsrooms have suddenly found themselves grappling with new forms of technology to produce significantly increased quantities and forms of content without extra staff. Time once spent chasing sources personally or by telephone has been diverted into producing several versions of the same story for different media. Meanwhile, the intricacies of crafting a memorable intro-duction or lead-in to a complex event or issue have been relegated in favour of uploading information in chunks and links, leaving the user to weave together the narrative for themselves from disparate sources.

Several high-profile and respected journalists have publicly condemned the manner of the shift to convergence in newsrooms. Among these is the investigative journalist David Leigh, assistant editor of the *Guardian,* whose own website attracts more than 18 million users a month, compared to an average readership of just over one million for the printed paper. At the inaugural Anthony Sampson lecture at City University, London, on November 1, 2007, he lamented:

> I fear that these developments will endanger the role of the reporter. Of course, there'll always be room for News Bunnies – to dash in front of a camera and breathlessly describe a lorry crash or to bash out a press-release in ten minutes. There'll probably be a lot more News Bunnies in the future – high-speed, short-legged creatures of the Internet Age. There will probably also be hyperlocal sites – postcode journalism fuelled cheaply by neighbourhood bloggers.

Leigh speaks for many within the industry, who worry that technology and the demand for high-speed instant news-as-it-happens will further erode the already-depleted resources provided by mainstream news organisations for investigative journalism. His views are backed by many in the US, such as Tom Grubisich who, in 2005, reviewed ten new citizen journal-ism sites and found many of them lacking in quality and content. (www.ojr.org/ojr/stories/051006). The leading academic, Nicholas Lemann, a professor in the prestigious Columbia

Journalism School in New York, has also expressed scepticism about the merits of online citizen journalism.

The issue of journalistic ethics looms especially large when untrained citizens try to report. News providers that take user-generated content publish guidelines on their sites, warning of health and safety, ethical and legal breaches but professional journalists say they do not go far enough. For example, when at the scene of an accident, trained journalists may have received rudimentary risk training, whereas a citizen journalist might put themselves in peril to capture the best footage, rather than helping the victims, or hamper the efforts of the emergency services. The lure of payment may tempt citizen journalists to trespass on private land or engage in criminal activity. Even in more mundane situations, a citizen reporter might invade privacy, intrude into someone's grief or harass celebrities. But even trained journalists breach ethical codes: professional status and experience does not necessarily guarantee appropriate behaviour. Ordinary citizens, who have not been inculcated in the competitive environment of the newsroom's culture may if anything be more sensitive to the predicament of potential sources, as they are not so far removed from there themselves.

Conclusion

The aim of the mainstream commercial journalism industry has, for the past 150 years at least, been to maximise audiences. Technological developments have aided and abetted that mission. The future of journalism in the digital age was demarcated a long time ago, as soon as the profit-motive began to loom large on the horizon. Given the speed with which they have transformed news, new technological developments have inevitably been met with concern but it is questionable whether they in themselves are the underlying cause of concerns and disharmony. Rather, it is the way in which these technologies have been introduced into newsrooms – and in many cases imposed on journalists by major news companies – that has caused significant consternation.

The future of journalism in the digital age, as in any age, is dependent on a solid commitment to upholding the highest news values, so that journalists, no matter whether they work in 'traditional' or new-fangled media, have the time and resources to carefully find sources, check their facts and interrogate issues of interest. Technology can both help and hinder that process. Many of the fears about a threat to standards from the rise of 'non-professional' journalists bear weight in the current context of efficiency drives in news organisations. But if skilled journalists are working to their fullest potential in investigating stories, public interaction and involvement should not hinder, and could in many ways enhance, the breadth and depth of their reporting.

If technology has given a stronger voice to the consumer of news, so that news values are brought to the fore, then technology can also provide the means for the ordinary citizen to intervene and hold journalism to account. The future of journalism in the digital age could be very positive indeed if we, as journalists and citizens, look under the thin veil of technological determinism at the real picture beneath.

6
Journalism during conflict

Journalists have long been players in the drama of conflict. They have been accused of helping to start wars, of ignoring them completely and of distorting public opinion through bias and propaganda. In 1898, jingoistic reporting was held partly responsible for the Spanish-American War. Seventy years later, journalists were held responsible for the lack of public support for the US effort in Vietnam. In the twenty-first century, there are concerns that the media have a symbiotic relationship with global terrorism. When opposing sides seek to control the media, information can be inaccurate or even censored. Yet, when a society is threatened by violent conflict, good journalism is vital in ensuring a plentiful supply of reliable information.

On the one hand, conflict appears to reflect a return to a primitive state. But on the other hand, the outcome of wars often depends on how they are perceived by the world, as well as how fiercely they are fought. The representation in the media of any side in a conflict can have a powerful impact on the responses of external agencies, such as governments, neighbouring factions, paramilitary groups and humanitarian aid agencies. It is no simple atrocity of war when the body of a captured soldier is dragged down the street – it will be filmed and released as a warning to the enemy's leaders.

Three factors have characterised the development of war coverage. First, technology has transformed the mediation of warfare, replacing the words and explanations of the war correspondent with live images beamed straight into the living room. War is shown to us, not explained to us. Second, our traditional perception of what wars look like has been transformed, most recently and acutely by global terrorism but also by civil wars and humanitarian crises. Third, war coverage is subject to the interests and interventions of many external forces: the military, governments and even humanitarian aid agencies can threaten the reporter's impartiality.

The war in Vietnam (1968–1975) made the role of the media in conflict a serious field of study in terms of its broader impact upon society. Since then, every conflict has provoked ever more debate on the impact of war reporting on our perceptions of reality and on our behaviour. It is therefore important to understand how war reporting has changed over time and to identify the structures and practices that affect war's coverage. Until recent years, in the West, conflict was something that happened far from home and its reporting reflected this. Today, as terror threats cause security alerts in airports, shopping centres and hotels, war correspondents might just as easily find themselves reporting from an urban street as from a remote mountainous region. The binary of 'them versus us', once the mainstay of war reporting, was completely upturned in the Balkans and by the 'War on Terror'. Modern conflicts have many stakeholders, each with their own 'truth', which presents many challenges for journalists. The coverage-garnering techniques used by agents in the field of war show that they are acutely aware of the transnational and global location of war and how the public can be influenced by the media.

In 1984, television footage shaped the international response to the war and famine in Ethiopia. Within ten years, the acknowledged effect of news reporting was a factor in the way the military prepared for battle in the Middle East and Eastern Europe, which led to fears that wars were being stage-managed to create the right media image. Journalists covering these conflicts were briefed on the latest manoeuvres in warehouse-sized media centres, rather than getting on to the battlefield. Twenty-four-hour rolling coverage of war, and more recently the Internet, has brought high-impact, startling and shocking live images of the aftermath of war to our television and computer screens.

Even as the media attempt to negotiate the ever-shifting forms and boundaries of global conflict, their performance is increasingly criticised. And in spite of concerns about journalistic propriety in war, there is a school of thought which suggests that the power of the media is indisputable and should be harnessed to help bring wars to an end. Given the complexity of the relationship between journalists and the conflicts they report, no consensus has been reached on whether reporters should be impartial onlookers or active agents. Advocates of media freedom defend journalists' right to report truthfully what they see rather than steer their coverage by a social aim. But the changing nature of conflict raises questions about whether established forms of war-reporting are relevant now that the underlying issues are so complex.

A short history of war reporting

Reporting about war has a long history: Julius Caesar was among the first to record his battles and Thucydides' *History of the Peloponnesian War* was based on his time in command of the Greek fleet (at Thasos in 424 BCE) and its subsequent defeat by the Spartan general, Brasidas. Over the centuries, war reporting has offered compelling and dramatic insights into human nature, how humans negotiate change and their fight for survival and supremacy and unflinchingly charted heroism, failures and the cost of war. War reporting embraces almost every essential news value – the unexpected, the dramatic, the emotive, the powerful – as it seeks to represent the unrepresentable. War coverage has myriad functions that go far beyond the imparting of facts (itself a difficult exercise in extreme conditions). It has to record for historical accuracy, yet be sensitive towards casualties and the families of serving military personnel. It must be careful not to prejudice soldiers' safety, while questioning the motives and actions of the military and governments. These aims have been fairly constant over the history of war reporting, although the idea of the independent eyewitness journalist is relatively recent.

Until the Crimean War of 1853, junior officers were the main recorders of information in battle. These soldier-reporters were more exposed to risk than are professional correspondents, but they did have unfettered access to the very heart of the struggle to aid their reporting. Their military sensitivities meant that they were very much their own censors, free from contemporary concerns that their output might cost lives, and largely beyond the pressures of deadlines or vested interests (bar the occasional court martial). They could take weeks to write their records, instead of having to report live even when little of moment was occurring. The fact that war stories sold more newspapers than anything else did not go unnoticed by the increasingly entrepreneurial editors of the late nineteenth century. *The Times* in London was among the first to abandon the practice of relying on irregular despatches from junior officers at the front. Its readers wanted to know what was happening day by day. Also, wars were getting bigger and lasting longer and editors felt carefully co-ordinated and trained reporters were needed overseas.

William Howard Russell, who covered the Crimean War for *The Times*, is often described as the first 'modern' war correspondent. The format of his and others' reports was very different from today's pithy summaries: a single report might be many thousands of words long and cover several pages. Stories from this era analysed battlefield strategy minutely and were published over many weeks – not until the telegraph became widespread were correspondents able to send daily reports. Events could be reported as they occurred but character-limits compelled that the copy filed was very concise. This set the pattern for today's 'inverted pyramid approach' (see Chapter 1).

In the Russo-Japanese War (1904–1905), press reporting was affected by restrictions on the movement of reporters and by strict censorship. The Japanese government attempted complete control of the press, urging journalists to act with patriotism. It also followed a hard line with foreign journalists, insisting that no information that might be useful to the other side was published. In all later military conflicts, the state sought to manage reporting. The First World War was the first modern mediated war and has parallels with the contemporary situation. The British Government established a Press Bureau during the conflict, to regulate the media and, as far as possible, prevent them serving as conduits of information about and between the warring states. The bureau aimed to project a positive image of Britain abroad and to encourage a unified national purpose. During this time the full horrors of war were not seen in the national press: there were no photographs of soldiers' bodies and discussion of shell-shock, military discipline and conditions in military hospitals and the trenches was avoided.

By the Second World War, hundreds of war correspondents and photographers followed every operation. The D-day landings, on June 6, 1944, had 558 accredited print and radio correspondents on the five Normandy beaches, but journalists in such numbers could barely navigate the hostile terrain and were greatly limited in what they could write. Numerous Allied reporters, photographers and camera operators went to Normandy but quickly found themselves engulfed for days and even weeks in the heavy fighting that followed the landings. This made transmitting stories quickly back to the home fronts difficult and the full horror of what happened at Omaha Beach took a very long time to become public. (Omaha was the most intensely fought-over beach on D-Day. The boats that delivered the American troops, amphibious Sherman tanks and weaponry halted too far out to sea. Not only did the tanks sink and take many men with them but surviving personnel in smaller boats were very exposed and denied the covering firepower needed to combat the German bombardment.) Journalists, such as the respected correspondents Ernie Pyle and Martha Gellhorn and the photographer Robert Capa, were restricted by censorship as well as by the German bombardments of the beaches. Military censors were beside the reporters as they went on to the beaches, monitoring their work to ensure that no one wrote or broadcast anything that might assist the enemy. But the military were also motivated by the need to sustain public support for the war.

Early film and television news rarely had war correspondents. Rather, they used film footage provided by other (often government) sources, to which the broadcaster added a voice-over. This footage was sometimes staged: cameras were large, bulky and difficult to move, compared to the very compact and mobile devices of today. One of the reasons that the Vietnam War changed public perception of the realities of war was the comparative ease of recording and transmitting footage. Damagingly for the US government, the full brutality of war became a nightly feature of the news. Smaller, better transmitters, videophones and portable computers mean that today, reporters can file copy or broadcast from anywhere in the world. Laptop computers have been used in war reporting since the 1980s but recent advances in portable satellite communication mean that footage can be transmitted instantly. Journalists previously had to rely on military support to gain access to transmission facilities, which carried the threat of censorship. This is not the case today.

Until the 1990s, television reports of wars were often fairly simple to understand. The wars had easily identifiable opponents, with fundamentally contrasting views on how society should be organised. Conflicts – whether physical or conducted through frosty diplomatic relations – were explained in simple terms: 'Communist', 'East/West' or 'coup'. To a greater or lesser extent, the context of most stories was whether the agents were supported in their actions by the Soviet Union or the United States. However, when war erupted in the former Yugoslavia and the Balkan states in the 1990s, it was neither easy for journalists to differentiate by placing the protagonists on the left/right spectrum, nor could they identify land ownership disputes or any other assets at the heart of the conflict. A changing world system, with social and economic shift in its wake, provoked people to turn upon the neighbours alongside whom they had once lived relatively harmoniously. This was very hard for journalists to explain in neat soundbites. There was no single truth, no consistent 'good versus bad' binary. And this 'Yugoslavian pattern' has subsequently characterised many wars across the globe.

The war in Bosnia, in 1993, caused a humanitarian crisis in the heart of southern Europe. More than a million people were displaced from their homes and needed emergency food and shelter. All economic activity stopped. Refugees in their thousands daily crossed into neighbouring countries or sought asylum in Western Europe. The humanitarian aid effort cost millions of dollars a day but at first no western government appeared willing to intervene militarily in the battle between Bosnians and Serbs. Instead, a mission aimed for a negotiated peace settlement and the mediators involved were anxious to ensure that reporting did not have a negative effect on the delicate negotiations.

The Bosnians and the Serb governments, and other agencies, each wanted the story told in particular ways. To bring in foreign support, the Bosnian government urged journalists to emphasise the moral elements of the story; and CNN's

Christiane Amanpour, one of the most famous journalists in the world, was accused of being partisan and pro-Bosnian. Keen to keep the Western military out, the Serbian government portrayed the conflict as insoluble. Pressure groups were eager to draw attention to human rights atrocities, to establish an international human rights law. Aid agencies were keen that the media not anger the Serb leadership, so that they could continue to support the displaced. Journalists faced many pressures, influences and viewpoints and were drawn into the conflicts and misrepresentations. The stakeholders' competing agendas meant one faction was always critical of media coverage.

The first Gulf War (August 2, 1990 – February 28, 1991) and the NATO operation in Kosovo (March – June 1999) were fought almost entirely from the air, using high-speed bombers armed with laser-guided bombs and missiles. Few correspondents got behind enemy lines and discovered how many were killed or injured and whether the bombers' targets were legitimate. There was no real battlefield: news reports were illustrated by military-supplied cockpit footage of night-time sorties striking enemy fortifications. Some journalists, including the BBC's John Simpson and Mike Williams and Paul Watson of the *Los Angeles Times*, managed to report independently and often heroically – but at great personal risk.

Some analysts and officials argue that the media – especially television – are the most powerful determinants of whether a nation will intervene in another's affairs. The former US Secretary of State, Madeleine Allbright, remarked during the Iraq War that CNN, due to the persuasive impact of its imagery, was like a sixteenth member of the UN Security Council. Live reporting on television and radio, and now online, means that journalists can vividly put events before their audiences before they have necessarily had time to make sense of it. The 1991 Gulf War was the first to be fought in the era of 24-hour television news: even when there was no new information to report, correspondents spoke on-screen with authority via briefings provided by their editors, several countries and thousands of miles away. Filling the airspace of rolling news means that military press conferences are often broadcast live and unmediated, leaving the audience to interpret the briefing without intervention or explanation.

The visual nature of the reporting has grown ever more dramatic, such as when crews based at CNN's Jerusalem and Tel Aviv bureaux in the Gulf War wore gas masks in a live broadcast during a suspected chemical weapons attack. In the invasion of Baghdad in 2003, the Allied Forces' press officers released unlikely-looking videogame-style footage of 'smart bombs' destroying military installations. And foreign journalists dodged missiles on hotel rooftops to deliver the most visually dramatic accounts. They could do this because they used highly-mobile satellite technology – although stories that the hotel-based journalists were briefed on events happening outside their door by their editors back home have circulated widely.

War reporting has a further ever-present struggle – the battle for power between the media and the military. While the journalist wants to reveal as much as possible about events, the military has always been reticent about its operations unless it has control over the message.

The propaganda problem

In 1918, Senator Hiram Johnson said that the 'first casualty of war is the truth'. To whom a war journalist is accountable can be an insurmountable difficulty and dilemma. Journalists under pressure are forced to decide whether their first duty is to truth or to their country. Governments in wartime have always used propaganda to maintain the morale of the armed forces and the public. It has also been used to intimidate the enemy by mobil-ising their own nation's dissent.

History reveals the emotive falsehoods of war: World War I German troops neither tossed Belgian babies in the air and caught them on bayonets nor boiled down German corpses for glycerine for munitions (a story invented by a British war corre-spondent). Iraqi soldiers invading Kuwait did not throw more than three hundred premature babies out of Kuwait City Hospital's incubators and leave them to die. This hugely-mediated story, said to be the testimony of a 15-year-old eyewitness, was reported in the *Sunday Telegraph* in London and then the *Los Angeles Times,* via a Reuters quote. It turned out to be propaganda, created by the pressure group 'Citizens for a Free Kuwait'. It took two years for the lie to be exposed, by which time the emotive story had served its function of hardening ordinary Americans' support of the invasion.

Journalists might argue that they are hardened to the techniques military officers and government spokespeople use when attempting to manipulate coverage. But developments during the GW Bush US presidency and Blair's period as British prime minister have shown the extent to which the authorities seek to frame news events positively. Video news releases (VNRs) are the latest strategy, in which governments attempt to 'place' ready-to-go footage in mainstream broadcasts.

In 2002, the British government launched a little-known television propaganda service that seems to mimic established systems in the US. The technology of journalism here offers a useful platform for the mediation of opinion as fact, either directly to audiences or through news outlets. British Satellite News (BSN) is produced in London by the corporate video and public relations firm, World Television, on behalf of the Foreign and Commonwealth Office. It is particularly aimed at overseas news organisations and seeks to present Britain in a positive light. BSN's website describes its service:

It supplies – free of charge – edited news material Monday–Friday to broadcasters around the world via global satellite distribution.

BSN concentrates on British Government policies and projects, British developments and news events; on the environment, climate change, science, technology, health and culture.

BSN supplies, via the internet and an e-mail service, scripts and shot lists to help TV broadcasters with each story.

The BSN website also shows news packages – voiced in English, Arabic and Spanish.

It is a unique service offering everybody the chance to see and hear the latest news from Britain.

The service is funded by the UK's Foreign and Commonwealth Office.

> www.bsn.org.uk/BSNJournalist/about.aspx?SiteId=
> Lw1T9rVFHwY%3d&locale=en-GB

'Embedding'

Observers have suggested that a mixture of co-operation and tension has historically characterised the relationship between the media and the military. The British military first developed 'embedding' in the 1982 Falklands War against Argentina. Because both the media and the military were so far from home, in the South Atlantic, journalists relied on the military not only for access to the battle zone but also for food, shelter and transmission of their reports. It is inevitable, in such difficult conditions, that journalists came to befriend soldiers. However, there is a concern that such close affiliation may lead to unbalanced, overly-sympathetic coverage and to dehumanisation of the opponent. The Falklands War has been described as the 'worst-reported war since the Crimean' in terms of military secrecy, censorship and technological limitations. There was no direct television transmission and no photographs for the first 54 days of the 74-day war and very long delays between action and reports reaching Britain.

More recently, governments have brought in systems of embedding journalists within military units that should, in theory, ensure first-hand eyewitness views of the action. During initial operations in Bosnia in 1995, the media were embedded within units in Germany to enable them to become familiar with servicepeople and to encourage a more sympathetic attitude toward the military. After conventional forces arrived in Afghanistan in 2002, a few American journalists were permitted to embed with ground forces for short periods. Journalists were also aboard the Navy aircraft carriers that supported the operation. In 2003, as the United States prepared to lead a coalition of countries into Iraq, its motives for invasion were seen as uncertain and unpopular. In response, the 'embedding' programme was developed, so that journalists could be immersed within military units, with direct access to the heroic, professional and human side of the military.

The benefit of embedding is to increase journalists' access to the front line but this is balanced by negative aspects. The main drawback is the lack of distance and independence between reporters and their protectors, which can affect the impartiality of their coverage. The coalition invasion of Iraq has been the most widely and closely reported war in military history. At the start of the war, in March 2003, nearly 800 reporters and photographers were travelling as 'embedded journalists' with US forces. The embedded reporters have to agree to several rules as they live with the soldiers and report on their actions. Before joining their battalions, the embedded journalists must sign a contract restricting when and what they can report. Details of military actions can be described only in general terms and journalists must agree not to write about possible future missions, classified weapons or information they might find. The commander of an embedded journalist's unit can declare a 'blackout', meaning the reporter is prohibited from filing stories via satellite. According to the Pentagon, blackouts are called for security reasons, as a satellite communication could tip off a unit's location to enemy forces.

MEDIA BLACKOUTS FOR FALLEN SOLDIERS

In April 2009, the media witnessed the return home of the body of a US soldier for the first time since the Pentagon had imposed a media blackout 18 years earlier. With the permission of his family, reporters watched the ceremony marking the return of the body of Air Force Staff Sgt Phillip Myers, killed by an improvised explosive device near Helmand province, Afghanistan.

The media ban was first put in place during the 1991 Gulf War. President George H W Bush, who implemented it, said it was necessary to protect the families of fallen soldiers. Critics of the ban always felt it was an attempt by the American government to disguise the human cost of the war from public opinion.

War coverage is not limited to 'embeds'. News organisations can and do send non-embedded reporters: 'unilaterals'. The military actively discourages unilaterals, warning that their safety during combat cannot be guaranteed. The dilemma for news outlets is that if they sign up to the embedding system, improved battlefield access and greater safety comes in return for accepting guidelines on reporting. Unilaterals are freer in their reporting but have limited access to soldiers and face more danger. Of the 14 journalists killed during the initial stage of the second Gulf War, nearly all were unilaterals.

Since the start of the twenty-first century, more than one thousand journalists and media personnel have been killed while working. World-wide, coping with harassment, intimidation, threats or worse has become an everyday part of a journalist's life. Iraq was, at the time of writing, the most dangerous place for journalists to work: since the war began in March 2003, more than 80 journalists and media workers have died there. Hundreds have been wounded – the ABC News anchor Bob Woodruff and the cameraman Doug Vogt were among the most high-profile cases. Dozens more have been abducted and some have been detained by the US military (according to statistics compiled by Reporters Without Borders and the Committee to Protect Journalists).

Violent attacks or imprisonment of journalists resonate deeply through the news industry and wider society. China and Cuba lead the world in imprisoning journalists. Attacks hamper journalists' ability to probe deeply and report accurately, which deprives the public of information. Article 19 of the UN's *Universal Declaration of Human Rights* (adopted on December 10, 1948 by a vote of 48 in favour, including the US and UK, with no objections and eight abstentions), states that journalists have the right to 'seek, receive and impart information'. This right is restated in the *International Covenant on Civil and Political Rights* which has been signed or ratified by more than 140 states, and in several regional conventions and charters, such as the *European Convention for the Protection of Human Rights* and the *African Charter of Human and Peoples' Rights*.

In times of peril, foreign correspondents increasingly rely on local contacts and freelance journalists to gather information on behalf of the Western media. The threat to foreign journalists is so acute in Iraq that much television coverage is gathered by locals. In Baghdad, Western journalists were often viewed as representatives of their home governments rather than independent, impartial eyewitnesses. War correspondents have always relied on local fixers to organise transport and interview opportunities but now it has become too dangerous to venture out, the local reporters themselves face grave risks. Journalists also face threats from other quarters, such as chemical or biological attack. The military has responded by giving accredited war correspondents hostile environment training, while the US Pentagon and the UK Ministry of Defence have offered journalists vaccinations against anthrax and smallpox.

TERRY LLOYD

Terry Lloyd, an ITN journalist, was found to have been unlawfully killed by American soldiers in southern Iraq. The inquest into his death heard that the troops shot the 50-year-old in the head while he was in a makeshift ambulance, having already been hurt in crossfire near Basra in March 2003. After the inquest, ITN's editor-in-chief David Mannion re-asserted the need for unilaterals, despite the real risks: ' Independent, unilateral reporting, free from official strictures, is crucial; not simply to us as journalists but to the role we play in a free and democratic society'.

Increased competition both within and between news organisations to be the first to report a story during a conflict means that media personnel are increasingly prepared to take risks in what are already dangerous environments. Some decline to travel with military personnel, instead opting for unarmoured four-wheel drive vehicles, marked with the word 'Press'.

Ethics of war reporting

Journalists face harrowing dilemmas in war coverage. Whether it is appropriate to step into the story to help someone is a key issue. To whom is the reporter responsible? Is it ethical to change from impartial observer to active agent? Much depends on whether journalists can feasibly be viewed as standing outside the action in the first place. Critics of the 'impartial' school believe that journalists should make 'social responsibility' their priority in the battle zone. The term can be loaded; certain regimes have used it to restrict media freedom. The contrasting view is that preserving media independence is ultimately in the public interest. Perhaps there are responsibilities that – as individuals and collectively – journalists ought to consider in war.

Critics of coverage of the first Gulf War and the Bosnian conflict often accused the news media of exaggeration, especially, in the latter case, of claims about the existence of concentration camps. The opposite accusation was made in Rwanda in 1994, when the international media were criticised for not identifying how widespread the killing was until it was too late. Over approximately 100 days, between the assassination of Juvénal Habyarimana on April 6 and mid-July, at least 500,000 Rwandan Tutsis were massacred by the Hutu militia. Estimates put the death toll between 800,000 and 1,000,000. The privately-owned pro-Habyarimana print media in Rwanda is believed to have started hate journalism against Tutsis but due to low levels of literacy, state radio had the biggest impact. Two key radio stations in the incitement of the violence before and during the genocide were Radio Rwanda and *Radio télévision libre des mille collines*. Radio Rwanda repeatedly broadcast a warning that Hutus would be attacked by Tutsis. Local officials used the message to convince Hutus that they needed to protect themselves by attacking first. Led by soldiers, Hutu civilians attacked and killed hundreds of Tutsis. The UN did not intervene until six weeks after the genocide began.

Some journalists were impelled to act on what they had witnessed first-hand. Lindsey Hilsum, a reporter for Channel 4 News in London, testified before the International Criminal Tribunal for Rwanda after witnessing mass killings. She acknowledged that this decision may have compromised her journalistic impartiality but felt this was outweighed by her responsibilities to her fellow humans. The journalistic community is split. Other journalists maintain that reporters must strive for complete moral detachment and simply reveal enough facts to allow the public and policymakers to form their own judgments. Jonathan Randal, a retired *Washington Post* journalist, refused to be questioned at the tribunal, saying it would endanger the lives of other correspondents. The court issued a summons but Randal, backed by the *Washington Post* and more than 30 international news organisations, has appealed against the decision.

Journalists may be able to exercise moral integrity in war reporting without compromising impartiality, yet still act in ways that might actively prevent suffering. One way is through the selection of stories and the news values ascribed to them. At any one time, dozens of conflicts may be occurring anywhere in the world and some are selected as news stories. This may be for operational reasons, as much as editorial preference. Covering foreign affairs can be hugely expensive; when a major war is under way in one region, a news outlet may ignore a smaller conflict (which was how Rwanda initially appeared to foreign observers) because it does not meet the news selection criteria.

Selection criteria in conflict journalism that will determine the billing of the item or promote news to the top of the agenda include factors such as whether the affected area has relevance to or connections with the home country, the involvement of any 'superpowers' or the home nation, the availability of strong audio or video and how much 'emotive' appeal there is in the conflict, such as an unfolding humanitarian disaster. The decision over whether or not to cover a story is framed by the availability of sources that ensure the conflict resonates with the reader and enables the audience to engage and identify with the struggle. A disaster borne out of civil war is likely to prompt appeals for funding by humanitarian aid agencies. This can be pivotal in getting the story covered, as it helps the reader to understand that they can personally make a difference by donating. Aid agencies also pay for journalists to travel to the scene of conflicts, to attract publicity. Due to tighter newsroom budgets, this is often the only way such events reach the public consciousness but the drawback is that the funding agency will direct the journalist towards promoting their organisations' priorities, which can affect the impartiality of the story. Going to the scene of a developing conflict and bringing it to the attention of the world before it deteriorates into full-scale war may be the ideal scenario but tight budgetary constraints mean this is less and less possible. If wars are to be prevented or settled, they first need to be recorded and understood, so that stakeholders have a sense of the issues involved, the potential risks and the prospects for peace.

The nature of modern conflict and its movement into the domestic sphere and communities mean journalists need to be carefully primed on how to act. Just as medical science has become more informed and intricate over the decades, so war reporting has become a specialised activity that requires an understanding of the multi-faceted nature of its participants including peacekeepers, charities and the modern military. Journalists need to mediate complicated causes and scenarios for their audiences and to represent what might turn out to be several different sides. Press reports are sometimes the only account of a conflict and can help researchers and policymakers improve their understanding and formulate strategies. One estimate is that in 2008 there were at least 15 wars happening around the world, claiming thousands of lives and innumerable casualties. Many of these conflicts have lasted longer than the World Wars of the twentieth century. Journalists' accounts have often been the only reliable data coming from these dangerous and remote areas.

The veteran BBC correspondent, Martin Bell, coined the term 'journalism of attachment' in calling for a different approach to reporting war. Journalism of attachment argues that reporters cannot remain detached or neutral in the face of modern evils like genocide in Bosnia or Rwanda but must side with the victims and demand that something is done. In the 1990s, one of the most admired foreign correspondents was Christiane Amanpour of CNN, a woman so sympathetic to the sufferings of the Bosnians that refugees chanted her name. 'In this war', she said:

> ... there was no way that a human being or a professional should be neutral. You have to put things in context. For me, objectivity does not mean treating all sides equally; it means giving all sides an equal hearing. It does not mean drawing a moral equivalent for all sides. I refuse to do that because I am going to report honestly.

> Cited by Harold Evans (2004) in 'Propaganda Versus Professionalism', British Journalism Review, 15 1 35-42

A problem with this approach is that it relies on there being a simple 'good' side with which to identify. Yet modern conflicts, not least in Bosnia, have shown with the passing of time, a more balanced picture emerges.

Peace journalism, now also referred to as 'conflict-sensitive' journalism, is another response to traditional reporting approaches but unlike the journalism of attachment it requires the media to remain neutral. Peace journalism aims to shed light on the structural and cultural causes of violence as they bear upon the lives of people in a conflict area and to frame conflicts as consisting of many parties, pursuing many goals, rather than a simple dichotomy. Those who advocate this approach claim that journalists need similar training to diplomats understanding the origins and causes of conflict. The nature of journalism is that it reports on the outward manifestations of conflict without exploring the causes and possible resolutions. However, it is argued, reporting the bare facts about violent conflict means that citizens will only be able to frame the conflict in violent terms and instead, journalists should report beyond the battle zone and garner opinions and experiences from many sources.

Ross Howard, a specialist in this field, has identified several ways in which journalism plays a key role in conflict resolution. First, journalists have a role to educate; reporting that delves into both sides' difficulties can help the opponent to understand their position better. Journalism can question perceptions and put disputes into context by reporting on how similar conflicts have been resolved elsewhere. Second, humanising the conflict by telling the story through the words of civilians and victims is one mechanism by which journalists foster engagement and identification in audiences thousands of miles away. It can also be used to humanise the parties involved in the dispute by profiling their real personalities, as opposed to showing them as mythical figureheads. Similarly, journalism offers catharsis and defuses aggression, by providing an emotional outlet for the aggrieved. Some reporters find it hard to consider being anything but an eyewitness, reporting what they see; they view conflict-sensitive reporting as active intervention in a story but its proponents argue that its fuller analysis preserves impartiality, by showing audiences the bigger picture.

Representing trauma – the media and terrorism

The media's coverage of conflict and humanitarian disasters is sometimes seen as pornographic in its cold explicitness. The graphic representation of tragedy can dehumanise the victims or cause the audience to avoid the story altogether. Knowing how much to convey and how to do it is difficult to judge. Journalists may feel it their duty to bear witness to war crimes and to bring them to the attention of the world. But they also have a responsibility to audiences – and simultaneously to victims and sources – not to repel them. They are under pressure from media owners to find angles and imagery that will help sell their products. Journalists face great difficulties in correctly balancing emotion and fact.

In the years since the 9/11 attacks on the United States, the world has become more uncertain and fearful. The declaration of a 'war on terrorism' by the United States and its international coalition has created a dangerous situation, in which journalists have become victims, as well as reporters, of events. The brutal killing of the *Wall Street Journal*'s correspondent, Daniel Pearl, in Pakistan early in 2002, which was filmed by his murderers, symbolises the distressing developments for journalism and freedom of expression. The terrorist attacks on the World Trade Center and the Pentagon were the most witnessed ever, relayed live by global media organisations to billions of viewers. Although this was a story that could not be ignored, journalism fuels terrorism through publicity. International terrorists want the greatest possible exposure for their actions and the relationship is symbiotic: the media cannot ignore atrocities on the scale of 9/11 or the London underground bombings of 2005.

Osama Bin Laden issued two videos in the wake of the World Trade Center attacks, broadcast by the Qatari television channel al-Jazeera. This shows how terrorist organisations do not just use the media to report the terrorist act: the videos demonstrated both the terrorists' reliance on the media and the media's role in reporting terrorism. The US government responded by warning news executives that the footage might contain coded instructions to others in Bin Laden's organisation. The broadcasters agreed to exercise caution in showing footage from the videos.

Terrorists' interest in mediation has significant implications for editorial judgment and independence. Editors may find their decision to publish or broadcast results in harm to innocent people. During the 1972 Olympics in Munich, members of the Israeli Olympic team were kidnapped and killed by Black September, an ultra-violent faction of the Palestine Liberation Organisation. The incident was seen on television by more than 900 million viewers. This was the first Olympics to take place after remarkable advances in technology. Portable cameras, video recorders and improved transmission mechanisms meant that the dramatic hostage-taking was broadcast immediately and in full colour by the hundreds of journalists covering the Olympics. The assault, and the nature of the Israeli response, thrust the Israeli–Palestinian crisis into the world spotlight, set the tone for decades of conflict in the Middle East and launched the new era of international terrorism. Disturbingly, it has been claimed the kidnappers knew where all the police snipers were because television stations showed their positions.

When news is live, editors balance their duty to report current events fully whilst still operating ethically. If a live hostage-taking were accompanied by demands to play a video message from the captors, should the journalist broadcast the message to spare the captive's life, or refuse to capitulate to terrorists? Ritual beheading is being used as a powerful instrument in the visual vehicle of war. Twenty-first century technology means that perpetrators of such crimes no longer need the media to circulate the images. 'Nick Berg' was the second most popular Internet search engine request in May 2004 (the television talent show *American Idol* was first), following the release on the Internet of a video of the American businessman's killing by Islamic militants. Not only television and the Internet were captivated by the demise of Nick Berg: a survey of 186 US newspaper front pages immediately after his death showed that 140 ran a sizeable image of Berg kneeling before his captors alongside the story. Of 125 foreign front pages studied, 28 published his image.

The two-week diplomatic struggle for the release of the British civil engineer Kenneth Bigley, kidnapped in Baghdad in 2004, was played out in a major media campaign, later criticised for giving too much airtime to the case of one man in many. Bigley was one of three captured engineers, frequently shown in video recordings pleading to the British Prime Minister, Tony Blair, to save his life and demanding the release of Iraqi women prisoners. Campaigners fighting for his release used the media to communicate to the captors that Bigley held an Irish passport. (Ireland did not support the Allied invasion of Iraq.) A video showing his killing was later posted on the Internet.

The aim of such violent videos, featuring the deaths of ordinary citizens, is to strike fear and cause havoc. Using the mass media ensures the terror is circulated as widely as possible. Senior news executives, who traditionally drew the line at depicting the most graphic war violence, now work in a media landscape where millions can instantaneously access unfiltered images on the Internet. Should media outlets limit themselves when they know the videos are widely available at the click of a mouse? The Arab television station al-Jazeera gained world-wide attention after 9/11 when it broadcast videos in which Osama bin Laden and his collaborators sought to justify the terrorist attacks on the United States. During the second war in Iraq, al-Jazeera angered the American and British coalition forces by broadcasting a 30-second film of the bodies of two dead British soldiers. Those who understood Arab culture pointed out that it did not share Western taboos on pictures of the dead: graphic footage of dead Palestinians and Israelis alike is a commonplace on Arab television screens. Al-Jazeera is routinely accused by the former US Defence Secretary, Donald Rumsfeld and others of 'consistently lying' and 'working in concert with terrorists'. The channel has attracted praise and derision in equal measure. On the one hand, it is seen as a healthy contrast to US channels such as Fox News, which overtly supported the Allied mission. On the other hand, giving airtime to Al Qaeda might be viewed as doing what the perpetrators of terrorism want.

Conclusion

Conflict reporting will inevitably continue to be a significant part of the media's staple fare. Climate change and economic uncertainty create the ideal conditions for war: resources are scarce, power is vested in a few hands and disagreements and misunderstandings can quickly escalate to violence, especially in remote regions. Technological advances have enabled journalists to report live from the scene of unfolding events but in many ways they have much less to report now than once they did. The very technology that should make journalism easier has been one of the key reasons the military has tightened its control over the movements of reporters. The complexity of modern conflict reporting seems to point to the need for further training and monitoring of journalists. By its very nature, conflict requires careful identification and understanding of the many positions and parties involved in a crisis. Journalists need to be very clear about their own role, including an acknowledgement that they are more than impartial witnesses to events. Conflict does not only happen 'abroad'; journalists can quite easily find themselves reporting from their own doorstep.

7
What is the future for journalism?

In the digital age, many uncertainties lie ahead for journalism. Despite huge transformations, we are probably far closer to the beginning of the online revolution than to its end. One might question whether it will end, as technology propels us into previously inconceivable domains. The future of journalism in the multi-platform, converged, media world is fraught with uncertainty. Discussion can only be based on opinion rather than on fact, and opinions diverge. One school of thought believes the significant decline in newspaper sales since the 1970s means newspapers will soon go out of business; a 'traditional' medium, relegated to the past. Alongside them, they fear, journalism – and its standards of accuracy and rigour – is also suffering from a terminal illness. Others say reports of the death of journalism are greatly exaggerated, for it is the 'content' that counts.

The emerging use of 'content' instead of 'news' or 'journalism' to describe material published, posted or broadcast has huge significance for both producers and audiences of journalism. 'Content' suggests that journalists' work is little more than 'stuff', filling a designated space, rather than the carefully-crafted result of quality reporting. It is interesting that it is the most threatened journalistic sector – newspapers – that is driving the change by adopting other forms of publishing; the Internet, audio and video. Broadcasting is experiencing its own problems, as audiences fall through the fragmentation brought about by the launch of digital services. But it is wrong to think that these changes are necessarily bringing down journalism, as many within the industry have argued. Technological developments can all too easily be made the scapegoat for something more insidious and damaging lying at the real heart of doubts about the future of journalism in the digital age.

Journalism faces many challenges but these have less to do with journalism, or even technology, than with the context within which journalism is produced. The economic basis of production has transformed both journalisms' processes and its perception by the public and institutions. This, more than anything, needs to be tackled if journalism is to survive and develop. Interactive media technologies present a golden opportunity for news-makers and news audiences to reflect on the present state of journalism. New formats and the reformulation of the relationships between reporters and readers offer a fresh challenge to long-held assumptions about what news is and the role of journalism in society. A challenge that, moreover, leads us urgently to revisit one of the most fundamental questions about journalism; a question which is as important to citizens as it is to reporters: what is news? Technology can serve as a catalyst for the debate.

The future's 'glocal'?

One of the under-promoted advantages – and under-used facilities – of the Internet is that it gives us access to content from newspapers, television channels, blogs and podcasts from around the world. We are no longer limited to local and national media to receive the news of the world; at the push of a button we can go directly to any corner of the globe and get the local angle.

In the mid-1980s, when computers revolutionised journalistic practices and transformed the economics of production and distribution, technology posed no threat to the media. Newspaper circulations had been in decline for the previous forty years, ever since television had started to play a central role in daily life. But television did not dent the appeal of journalism. If anything, it raised the media's global profile. While television supplied visually-impressive footage, newspapers understood their role within the burgeoning journalism marketplace: the delivery of broad coverage, deep analysis and opinion. The digital revolution, which allows words, pictures and sound to be delivered to home computers and hand-held devices, offers a limitless increase in the amount of information. This is not so much a threat to journalism as a challenge. Some journalists are pessimistic about the new forms and their perceived threat to standards but globally, the future of journalism looks buoyant.

The Paris-based World Association of Newspapers (WAN) collates annual data collected from 216 countries. These data show that in 2006, global newspaper sales were 2.3% higher than in the previous year and had risen 9.5% over the previous five years. If free-distribution daily newspapers are added to the figures, the growth rates are nearly doubled. In recent years, in highly-developed markets such as the US and UK, newspaper circulation has been steadily decreasing but that local situation cannot be said to mirror global or even European trends.

The upsurge in journalism consumption has been bolstered by major circulation growth in the five years from 2002–07 in the burgeoning new economies of India (up by just under 54%) and China (up 15.5%). In Europe, the press in Italy, Portugal, Austria and Ireland performed well, despite the fact that Internet use is high. World-wide, in 2007, 515 million readers bought a newspaper every day, compared with 488 million in 2002. As newspapers are often shared, average daily readership is probably around 1.4 billion. Consumers of news are not necessarily switching to the Internet, even when it is close to hand but expanding their interest in news by exploring a far wider range of outlets.

'Top-down' to 'bottom-up'

Greater and greater interactivity means that online writing tends to be more personal, giving reporters, editors and news anchors the chance to be more human and connect with their audience in deeper ways. This can be very challenging to traditionalists. History shows that media organisations embrace technology to increase efficiency, reduce costs and maximise audiences but there is evidence that recent developments may – ironically – have the potential to wrest some of that power from the corporations. In the early twenty-first century, networked computers, digital cameras and mobile telephones with multiple functions are affordable by ordinary consumers. Digital content, capable of being used across media platforms, can be produced by ordinary citizens as well as professional news gatherers. The public can take a very different and active role within the news-making process, seeking alternative news sources, actively providing content or through other new and emerging means. This reconfigures the relationship between journalism and its audiences and raises important questions about its role, status and function in society.

Mass communication has traditionally been 'top-down': a 'few' mediating to the 'many'. In contrast, digital journalism, such as news websites and blogs, mean online news has the scope to be a two-way conversation between news producer and news receiver. Audiences enter into dialogue with news providers, rather than being passive partakers. Readers of interactive online news are free, within editorial constraints, to select the stories they wish to read, investigate them in how much depth they want and, potentially, respond to them. Increasingly – and most significantly – news receivers are being invited to share in producing the news content, taking on some of the functions of journalists by circulating information, images, video footage, audio clips and text.

New technology could revolutionise investigative journalism. Increasing pressure on news outlets to be fast and first means that journalism, which is both expensive to produce and time-consuming to gather, has a much lower priority. This, coupled with a move away from factual to entertainment and reality programming on television, means the outlook is not rosy for investigations in the 'traditional' media. Some hope that the Internet, and the closer rapport it engenders between journalists and their audiences, might serve to regenerate in-depth reporting. Such collaborative investigations are made possible by easy communication and experiments such as newAssignment.net. This site, which was launched by the media commentator Jay Rosen in 2006, aims 'to spark innovation in "open platform" journalism, distributed reporting and what's now called crowdsourcing'. For example, The Sunlight Foundation gave tools to citizen journalists so they could find out which members of US Congress employed their spouses, the *Los Angeles Times* and amateur investigators worked together to unmask the *LonelyGirl15* video actress, Jessica Rose and the *Huffington Post* joined with *Off The Bus* to create a site for 'ground level'

FOOT-AND-MOUTH

During the 2001 foot-and-mouth crisis in the UK, anyone wanting up-to-the-minute authoritative information turned to the blog warmwell.com. The site was established in May by a British woman, Mary Critchley. It had a daily summary of as many newspaper reports as possible on the progress of the crisis, offered farmers legal advice about their rights, provided a place for people to express their disquiet and, very importantly, published the views of vets and scientists who dissented from the policies adopted by the UK authorities. (The most controversial and harrowing policy was to cull more than six million livestock as a contingency measure to stop the virus spreading.) The site quickly found an audience and, in the same way as in the London bombings, citizens affected by the story played a significant part in its chronicling.

reporting in the 2008 US election campaign. Although it is often viewed as a challenge to the traditional news media, the Internet might better be conceptualised as their complement – supplementing and interconnecting the work of professional journalists with that of citizens.

Web-based citizen investigations can serve as a catalyst prompting fuller coverage from mainstream outlets. In investigations, citizen journalism has the potential to be, as one commentator described it, 'People who are non-journalists committing random acts of journalism'. (blog.seattletimes.nwsource.com/presshere/2008/01/theres_a_news_war_going.html) Citizen journalists can also be thought of as one stakeholder in a wider movement for the democratisation of the media. In many respects, online journalism brings us closer to a vision of the public sphere in which citizens have a full and informed debate in the interests of democracy.

Greater checks and balances on mainstream sources

In the past, if you wanted to comment on a story that had been broadcast or published, correct a fact or add additional information, you either had to work at a mainstream news organisation or send in a letter and hope it was selected. Now, outsiders and experts exert their influence over the news agenda. Not only does this offer a diverse array of viewpoints but it may also take the agenda-setting power out of the hands of a few and into those of the many.

Another benefit is that there are more fact-checkers than ever. Citizens and bloggers provide an important check on stories and bring a new diversity to reporting. They might be biased but their passion for an issue may reveal inaccurate reporting, missed angles and misrepresentation.

SWITCHING OFF THE FEEDBACK LOOP

Shortly after the murder of the Pakistani opposition party leader Benazir Bhutto in December 2007, BBC journalists uploaded the story on to the corporation's award-winning news website. As commentators and spokespeople speculated that certain Islamic opponents of Mrs Bhutto might be behind the killing, website users began to post their feedback, using the *Have Your Say* forum. Days later, the BBC's then Head of News, Peter Horrocks, revealed that his interactive team had considered switching off the facility on the forum that allowed users to recommend their favourite feedback comments. Many of the top 20 recommended posts were damning of Islam, something which caused journalists and moderators great concern and difficult editorial judgements. Horrocks later reflected: 'It was only a fleeting suggestion but that we could consider, however briefly, freezing this important part of the BBC News service tells you something about the power and the potential danger of the new intensity of the interaction between the contributing public, journalists and audiences'. This example is one of many happening every day in the media that highlight the issues arising from the rapid development and wide-scale deployment of interactive news-making.

Interactivity will clearly compromise broadcasting's future impartiality severely. Section 4 of the BBC's Editorial Guidelines: Impartiality & Diversity of Opinion states that:

Impartiality lies at the heart of the BBC's commitment to its audiences. It applies across all our services and output, whatever the format, from radio news bulletins and our web sites to our commercial magazines and includes a commitment to reflecting a diversity of opinion.

When the public can easily access a wide range of views through the Internet, it is increasingly likely that they will turn away from broadcasters who fail to encompass their personal views in their output. This is less of a problem for newspapers and independent websites which are allowed to adopt clear editorial standpoints, which might open the way for newspapers to capitalise on their unique potential as 'viewspapers'; papers that follow a clearly partial editorial line.

This has led senior broadcasters to propose, controversially, that the BBC embrace the idea of 'radical impartiality', in which public service broadcasters would accommodate the dissemination of a broader range of views. But, Horrocks writes: 'views that are rigorously tested but with respect for all legally expressed opinions'. This stance deviates little from present editorial impartiality guidelines, which mandate the representation of a wide array of voices. Furthermore, Horrocks focuses heavily on comment pages, which may be accessed by only a small proportion of the BBC audience. Surely the aim should be to encourage more and more feedback from and engagement with news audiences, who may shape the agenda and potentially provide an important 'check and balance' on the quality and truth of the news?

Before stepping down as prime minister, Tony Blair made a speech criticising the British media, during which he singled out the *Independent* newspaper as a 'metaphor' for what happened to the news during his tenure, saying it was 'well-edited and lively' but 'avowedly a viewspaper not merely a newspaper'. The paper's striking images and powerful headlines undoubtedly catch the eye on news–stands and get to the root of issues in an accessible manner. The 'red issue' of May 2006, guest-edited by Bono from U2, was perhaps the most famous of the *Independent*'s front pages, and drew attention to what some see as the skewed news values of many media outlets. It combined the headline 'No news today' in yellow text on a red background with a much smaller subheading at the bottom of the page, which read, 'Just 6,500 Africans died today as a result of preventable, treatable disease'. The editor, Simon Kelner, has moved on and the issue-based front pages have departed with him. But the strong editorial line might have left a legacy, by reminding us of what advantages newspapers have.

If a newspaper is to distinguish itself from online competitors, even from its own website, its position to comment, analyse and offer lengthier prose could be exploited. Newspapers must ask themselves what they can provide that people are willing to pay for. The barrier that has separated fact from opinion and hallmarked newspaper journalism for almost a century can never be breached, according to traditionalists. But with so much real-time news available free on the web, are newspapers wasting their time continuing as the primary news providers? Selecting and explaining key news items would appear to be a sensible shift for the industry.

If the changes in newspaper formats over the past decade are analysed, this step would be much less radical than it sounds. It may be used to enhance the 'page one' splash through feature journalism or carry an off-beat or human interest piece. Newspapers, it is clear, have been steadily reducing their news budgets and origination of exclusive material. The word count of any quality weekend newspaper is probably equivalent to a couple of novels, a lot of it of the lifestyle genre. Supplements on health and beauty, sport, travel, motors and homes, CDs and DVDs, spill out of plastic bags on Saturday and Sunday mornings. Internet browsers are unlikely to stumble across comment pieces that might challenge their perceptions unless they actively seek them out. In the pluralistic press, they are delivered straight to them.

News for free

Regardless of format, traditional media have to change to attract new audiences, usually younger than their established audience.

The use of online media, and the consequent decline in use of 'traditional' media, is widely believed to be most prevalent in the young. The 18- to 35-year-old generation, who've grown up with the World Wide Web, expect to get their news for free. They get it from television, in their e-mail inboxes, on their phones – all at the click of a button. The UK's media regulator, Ofcom, found data to support this expectation in its 2006 report. Younger consumers spent more time on the Internet than reading newspapers and magazines or tuning into television and radio and while 14% of media consumers of all ages said they read national newspapers less since they started using the Internet, that figure rose to 27% among 15–24 year olds. However, the message from Ofcom was not that traditional media would become redundant but rather, that to survive, they would need to change and adapt.

There is considerable current debate about free newspapers and the possibility that they will rejuvenate a flagging industry. In his recent book *The Vanishing Newspaper*, Philip Meyer calculated that 2043 will be the year when newsprint dies in America, 'as the last exhausted reader tosses aside the last crumpled edition'. Newspapers that seek to rival the Internet or broadcasting as the first source of news are unlikely to be bought when free versions are available, especially by younger people. Papers may have to be creative about changing the relationship between their print and online formats. For example, many newspaper websites simply upload the text of the print version, albeit with a few interactive features. Many publishers feel print has a more hallowed authority and should be treated as their main output. Perhaps this should be reversed, for free newspapers could attract greater numbers of younger people to news. Free newspapers have the power to promote a paid-for or subscription-based news website and to lead readers to fuller content on a free site that attracts plenty of advertising. Free newspapers have been criticised for their concision and lack of original reporting. But this might be ideal if they directed the reader towards richer reportage on the web.

Significant challenges lie ahead, which could delimit or jeopardise journalism's future health. A series of scandals, such as the Jayson Blair fabrications for the *New York Times*, combined with concern over media monopolies has, without doubt, challenged the public trust in journalism. Intrusion, dumbing down and 'infotainment' are but a few of the factors that have led to calls for the industry to exhibit greater transparency. One result has been a widening disconnection between the public and journalism, evident in the shifting public image of the journalist in opinion polls and in popular culture. Think how journalists were once portrayed in the cinema. From the wise-cracking Hildy in *His Girl Friday* to Clark Kent and Lois Lane in *Superman*, journalists were crusading, wise-cracking public servants, working for the good of society. Today, the public has withdrawn its affection, lampooning the seemingly vacuous, image-obsessed nature of the corporate, professional self-seeking journalist, epitomised by Courtney Cox's Gale Weathers in the *Scream* trilogy. Maintaining the public's faith in journalism as a watchdog for democracy, rather than as entertainment, is vital if the industry is to maintain public faith.

The reduction of the public faith in journalism has been accompanied by the breakdown of another important relationship; one far more threatening to journalistic standards than technology. Media owners and journalists once worked in close union, with a common purpose of producing news that would attract as many readers, listeners and viewers as possible. Journalism, it was felt by both, was the lifeblood of the industry and to dilute the content would not only lose audiences but also the reputation of the industry as a whole.

In recent years, a noticeable distance has developed between media proprietors, journalists and audiences, coincidental with the shift from strong publishers and campaigning moguls to executive boards and shareholders. This breakdown of relationships seems to have occurred when small outlets, run by local owners, were sold to corporations. This brought newsrooms better facilities and offices and more efficient production and infrastructures. But as years went by, the nature of the journalism business underwent a dramatic transformation. Power once vested in the heads of corporations became a need to maximise investors' returns. Owners, even when they were chairing a board, were identifiable and personified the ideology of the operation. Today, with one or two notable exceptions, such as Rupert Murdoch's empire, the ownership of a corporation is amorphous and de-personified, which has a knock-on effect on journalists.

Journalism is felt, by the majority of its practitioners, to be a source of identity and a vocation as much as a business or profession. People tend to be drawn to the trade or craft from human curiosity and a desire to engage actively in the making of history and its mediation to as wide an audience as possible. Journalism has never been a particularly well-paid or family-friendly occupation, requiring its practitioners to work round the clock, often in difficult conditions, with a strong element of unpredictability and risk. But camaraderie exists between journalists, a shared, almost unspoken, understanding of their field and its pressures. However, the bonds that once existed between journalists and their organisations are gradually being eroded. Only a few journalists are now lucky enough to enjoy a secure job for life, working for an outlet that they love. For most, the job has become short-term contracts, casual shifts and uncertain freelance work, which hardly fosters connections between immediate colleagues, let alone with the journalistic mission of a single organisation.

Cost-cutting has reduced the number of correspondents stationed abroad, shrivelled or closed news bureaux and crippled local reporting staff who once kept an eye on governors, mayors, councillors, criminals and the justice system. It has shrunk the size of the typical newspaper page, cutting the cost of newsprint but reducing news content. This is damaging for morale which will be, in turn, detrimental to the future of journalism. That so many outlets are fighting for their survival suggests that free-market capitalism is not the ideal platform on which to base the journalism industry.

As the conventional business model for commercial journalism is put under greater threat, some outlets are backed by non-profit organisations. A few respected news organisations sustain themselves in this way, including the *Guardian* in the UK and the *Christian Science Monitor* and National Public Radio in the US. It is also happening locally in Britain, where local authorities are publishing free-distribution newspapers to promote their work and inform a public starved of council coverage, albeit uncontroversially.

Branded content – news as commodity

While no-one can predict how technology and businesses will intertwine and enable journalism to recover its footing, one thing is certain: brand identity will become essential in promoting media products and increasingly important to publishers and broadcasters wishing to preserve the integrity of their products as they negotiate technological shifts. As the industry grapples with how websites and interactivity should work, they can at least work towards maintaining and promoting faith in the integrity of their brand of journalism.

Magazines have always been good at branding and some areas of the periodical market have experienced considerable growth and buoyancy, while others have floundered. This sector is adept at identifying fresh markets and forging a rapport with its readers, whether they comprise US women in their twenties and thirties or British undertakers! When readers are satiated and starting to move on, magazine publishers unhesitatingly close the title and launch a fresh product for a brand-new demographic. Periodicals have achieved this market insight through detailed research into the lifestyles, tastes and habits of their readers and have adjusted their content accordingly.

The same approach has been adopted by newspapers in the late 1990s and early 2000s in pursuit of younger, more affluent readers and to boost circulations and offer a more lucrative audience to their advertisers. It is evident in the rise of the newspaper 'design director', who ensures that the layout, typography, colours, paper stock and image choices fit the identity of the target readership. The target readership is not necessarily the actual readership but is implied through aspirational features such as holiday reviews, fashion pages and home interiors sections. These design-based, demographic-led decisions frame the way the journalism is 'branded' to make it a product that fits with the overall consumption tastes of the implied reader. The selection of stories, the vocabulary, the word length and the size and boldness of headlines can be determined by this notion of what the target reader 'wants'.

Considering that the sales of the popular press are in greatest decline, the message seems to be that news consumers are looking for a brand they can trust to deliver the content. More investment in innovation, quality and rigorous reporting might lure audiences back to journalism, which in turn may bring back the advertisers who are currently promoting themselves in non-journalistic outlets. The alternative is to find a completely different funding model.

Conclusion

We can only speculate what the future of journalism holds. The history of journalism helps us to understand that news, far from being something reported objectively from a 'real' world, is inextricably connected to the development of society, politics, industry and culture. Journalism has to be viewed as a reflection of everyday life, framed by institutions and contexts that also shape the lives of readers and audiences. The content of newspapers, magazines, bulletins and websites is not produced in an hermetically-sealed environment. While journalists strive for independence from state interference or intrusive proprietors, they remain members of society, subject to the ebbs and flows in their environment and culture.

The routine practices of news editors and reporters were not invented in one fell swoop. They arose and evolved from particular circumstances and philosophies. And they are still arising and evolving, thanks to the opportunities that technology is bringing. The debates about journalism's future are interesting and significant, as stakeholders seek to form a relationship with the new formats on offer. The industry is embracing interactive journalism, as shown by the fact that virtually all mainstream news organisations in the UK have some kind of online presence; it is the journalists themselves who are wary about the new online environment but in the future, as has been proven in the past, they will find a way to accommodate these changes for the benefit of the public interest.

Whether the journalist is expressing their views through a long editorial in a quality newspaper or pushing the button on a twenty-word 'tweet', good journalism should be the overarching priority, whatever technology is used to publish it. Digital developments have arisen amid burgeoning media consolidation and mergers and at a time when corporations allow a news-as-commodity approach to dominate production values and editorial strategies. The Internet and its associated journalisms are trying, albeit haphazardly, to fill a gaping news chasm which opened long before the first website was launched, the first podcast uploaded and the first blog posted. They are an

important reminder that journalism has always been an annoy-
ance, a scurrilous activity, operating on the borders of society, in
dark recesses where ordinary people fear to delve. Its practitioners have never done the job to be liked or admired. Surely it is
inevitable that good journalism will seek to unpack its own
processes and expose their limitations. By undercutting the
corporatisation and professionalisation of journalism, these new
models offer some interesting glimpses into a journalism free of
outside constraints.

It is very appropriate that the title of this book is *A Beginner's
Guide* ..., for it proposes that we may be at the start of a new
journey.

Further reading

Chapter 1

Curran, J and Seaton, J (2003) *Power Without Responsibility*, Routledge

Chapman, J (2005) *Comparative Media History*, Polity

Conboy, M (2004) *Journalism: A Critical History*, Sage

Crook, T (1997) *International Radio Journalism*, Routledge

De Beer, A and Merrill, J (2003) *Global Journalism*, Allyn and Bacon

Harcup, T (2004) *Journalism: Principles and Practice*, Sage

Mill, JS (1989) *On Liberty*, Cambridge University Press

Pilger, J (2005) *Tell Me No Lies: Investigative Journalism and its Triumphs*, Vintage

Wolfe, T (1973) *The New Journalism*, Pan

Chapter 2

Boyd-Barrett, O and Rantanen, T (1998) *The Globalization of News*, Sage Publications

Herbert, J (2001) *Practising Global Journalism: Exploring Reporting Issues Worldwide*, Focal Press

Hicks, W and Holmes, T (2002) *Subediting for Journalists*, Routledge

Machin, D and Niblock, S (2006) *News Production: Theory and Practice*, Routledge

Randall, D (1999) *The Universal Journalist*, Pluto

Chapter 3

Curran, J and Seaton, J (2003) *Power Without Responsibility*, Routledge

Doyle, G (2002) *Understanding Media Economics*, Sage

Doyle, G (2002), *Media Ownership*, Sage

Ginneken, J (1998) *Understanding Global News*, Sage

Keane, J (1991) *The Media and Democracy*, Polity

McManus, J (1994) *Market-Driven Journalism: Let the Citizen Beware?*, Sage

Page, B (2003) *The Murdoch Archipelago*, Simon and Schuster

Shawcross, W (1992) *Murdoch*, Chatto and Windus

Tumber, H (2000) *Media Power, Professionals and Policies*, Routledge

Chapter 4

Clayton, R (2001) *Privacy and Freedom of Expression*, Oxford

Feintuck, M (1999) *Media Regulation, Public Interest and the Law*, Edinburgh

Gallant, S and Epworth, J (2001) *Media Law*, Sweet and Maxwell,

O'Neill, O (2004) *Rethinking Freedom of the Press*, Royal Irish Academy

Robertson, G and Nicol, A (2007) *Media Law*, Sweet and Maxwell

Chapter 5

Allan, S (2006) *Online News: Journalism and the Internet*, Open University Press

Axford, B and Huggins, R (2001) *New Media and Politics*, Sage

Campbell, V (2004) *Information Age Journalism*, Edward Arnold
Gillmor, D (2006) *We The Media: Grassroots Journalism By The People, For the People*, O'Reilly Media
Herbert, J (2000) *Journalism in the Digital Age*, Focal Press

Chapter 6

Allan, S and Zelizer, B (2005) *Reporting War: Journalism in Wartime*, Routledge
Knightley, P (2000) *The First Casualty*, Prion Books
Shaw, M (1996) *Civil Society and Media in Global Crises: Representing Distant Violence*, Continuum
Thussu, D and Freedman, D (2003) *War and the Media*, Sage
Tumber, H and Palmer, J (2004) *Media at War*, Sage
Tumber, H and Webster, F (2006) *Journalists Under Fire*, Sage

Chapter 7

Boczkowski, P (2005) *Digitising the News*, MIT Press
Cottle, S (2003) *News, Public Relations and Power*, Sage
Davies, N (2009) *Flat Earth News*, Vintage
Franklin, B (1997) *Newszak and News Media*, Edward Arnold
Meyer, P (2004) *The Vanishing Newspaper: Saving Journalism in the Information Age*, University of Missouri Press
Paterson, C and Sreberny, A (2004) *International News in the 21st Century*, Libbey & Co.

Index

A Beginner's Guide to Censorship

9781851686742
£9.99/ $14.95

Offering a potted history of the phenomenon from the execution of Socrates in 399BC to the latest in internet filtering, Petley provides an impassioned manifesto for freedom of speech. Also explaining how media monopolies and moguls censor by limiting what news/entertainment they impart, this is an invaluable resource for anyone interested in global media in the information age.

"This is an important and timely book and I recommend it to anyone who thinks that censorship belongs to the pages of history." *Tribune*

"An essential read for anyone concerned about this curiously neglected area of media scholarship. A timely reminder about the dangers of censorship for democratic societies." **Bob Franklin**, Professor of Journalism Studies, Cardiff University

JULIAN PETLEY is professor of Film and Television at Brunel University. He is the author of several books on censorship, and has written for the *Guardian* and the *Independent*.

Browse further titles at
www.oneworld-publications.com

Blackpool Sixth *Beginners*
FYi Library **GUIDES**

01253 394911
fyi@blackpoolsixth.ac.uk